LIFE

ALBUM

1995

Pictures of the Year

LIFE ALBUM
1995
Pictures of the Year

EDITOR Melissa Stanton

SENIOR WRITER Kenneth Miller　　**DESIGNER** Marti Golon

DEPUTY PICTURE EDITOR Adrienne Aurichio

WRITERS Nikki Amdur, Harriet Barovick

ASSISTANT DESIGNER Jean Andreuzzi

ASSISTANT PICTURE EDITORS Maggie Berkvist, Azurea Lee Dudley, Vivette Porges

RESEARCH Romy Pokorny　　**TECHNOLOGY** Steve Walkowiak
And all members of the **LIFE COPY DEPARTMENT**

ASSISTANT MANAGING EDITOR Susan Bolotin

DIRECTOR OF DESIGN Tom Bentkowski　　**PICTURE EDITOR** Barbara Baker Burrows

---

TIME INC. NEW BUSINESS DEVELOPMENT

DIRECTOR David Gitow

ASSOCIATE DIRECTOR Stuart Hotchkiss

ASSISTANT DIRECTOR Pete Shapiro

FULFILLMENT DIRECTOR Mary Warner McGrade

DEVELOPMENT MANAGERS Bob Fox, John Sandklev

OPERATIONS MANAGER John Calvano

PRODUCTION MANAGER Donna Miano-Ferrara

ASSOCIATE DEVELOPMENT MANAGERS Mike Holahan, Allison Weiss

ASSISTANT DEVELOPMENT MANAGER Dawn Weland

MARKETING ASSISTANT Charlotte Siddiqui

Books

Copyright 1996
Time Inc. Home Entertainment
Published by LIFE Books
Time Inc.
1271 Avenue of the Americas
New York, NY 10020

ISBN # 1-883013-08-9
Printed in the United States of America
First edition
"LIFE" is a registered trademark of Time Inc.

PICTURE SOURCES are listed by page. 6: JB Pictures. 8: The Boston Globe. 10: Sygma. 12: Gamma Liaison. 14: AP. 16: AP. 18: Argus Leader. 20: Newsday. 22: AP. 50-51: Clockwise from top left: Tom Rodriguez/Globe Photos; John Paschal/Celebrity Photo; Cindy Karp/Black Star; Steve Granitz/Retna Ltd.; Steve Granitz/Retna Ltd.; Malcolm Clarke/Retna Ltd.; Steve Granitz/Retna Ltd.; Frank Trapper/Sygma; Berliner/Gamma Liaison; Lester Sloan/Gamma Liaison; Jim Smeal/Ron Galella Ltd.; Barry King/Gamma Liaison; Lisa Rose/Globe Photos. 60: top: Davis Factor/Visages; bottom, left to right, Steve Finn/Alpha-Globe Photos; Lisa O'Connor/Celebrity Photo; Jim Smeal/Galella Ltd.; Mitch Gerber/LGI. 61: left, top to bottom, John Barrett/Globe Photos; Lisa Quinones/Black Star; Andrea Renault/Globe Photos; Photofest; right, Stephanie Pfriender/Outline Press. 78-79: clockwise from left, AL/Ramey Photo Agency; Richard Chambury/Alpha-Globe Photos; David McGough/DMI; Marcel Thomas/Sipa Press; Neal Preston/Retna Ltd.; Bebeto Matthews/AP; Guy Webster; John Roca/New York Daily News; Russ Einhorn/Gamma Liaison. 96-97: clockwise from left, Ramey Photo Agency; Jim Smeal/Galella Ltd.; John Barrett/Globe Photos; Lisa Rose/Globe Photos; Jeff Christensen/Gamma Liaison; Harry Benson; Alexandra Boulat/Sipa Press; Lisa Rose/Globe Photos; Anthony Savignano/Galella Ltd. 106: left to right, top to bottom, Sygma (2); Andrew Taylor/Photoreporters (2); Pool/Gamma Liaison; Pool/Sygma. right, Harry Benson. 107: clockwise, Ken Lambert/Washington Times-Gamma Liaison; Houston Chronicle; Richard Drew/AP; Najlah Feanny/Saba; Steve Ueckert/Houston Chronicle; Sygma. 136: clockwise from top left, Ken Regan/Archive Photos; Blake Little/Sygma; CBS; Visages. 137: bottom left, Rick Friedman/Black Star; center top, Bill Nation/Sygma; center bottom, David Sprague/Sygma; top right, Marc Bryan-Brown.

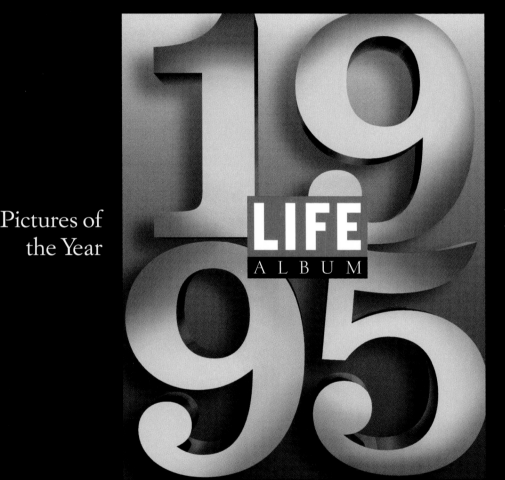

Pictures of
the Year

LIFE
ALBUM

19
95

By the
of LIF

Contents

A monstrous and marvelous year

T hings fall apart; the center cannot hold"—so wrote William Butler Yeats in *The Second Coming,* his famous indictment of a change-mad age. But the Irish poet and prophet got it only half right: Things also fall together, often drawn by the same forces—technological, cultural, political—that propel them toward division and decay. This year, Americans traded fire from behind the color lines over the murder trial of O.J. Simpson, yet they joined hands to try to pull Colin Powell into the presidential race. A bombing in Oklahoma City revealed the depth of the country's ideological chasms, but the explosion's aftermath proved the strength of human bonds. The assassination of Israel's chief peacemaker spurred peace talks with Syria. The Bosnians stopped fighting. Cal Ripken Jr. kept playing. And though the Internet often closeted its devotees in lonely rooms, it linked minds and hearts throughout cyberspace. (It also inspired a thriller called *The Net,* giving filmgoers a chance to commune with Sandra Bullock, girl-next-door of the moment.) Yeats spoke, in his apocalyptic poem, of a "rough beast . . . [that] slouches toward Bethlehem to be born"—and certainly, as the millennium approaches, assorted monsters are arising among us. To some, the year's proposed megamergers might qualify: Chase and Chemical, ABC and Disney, Westinghouse and CBS, Time Warner and Turner Broadcasting. (The self-dismemberment of AT&T struck employees threatened with layoffs as monstrous in another way.) Yet many of the "mergers" of 1995—foam dancing, coed cigar parties, macho movie stars in drag—were playful rather than baleful. To see the year in all its beastliness and beauty, as only LIFE can show it, just turn the page.

Just trying to live …

BLOOD AND HOPE

As Serb snipers and shellfire filled Sarajevo's graveyards, children in the Bosnian capital found ways to be children despite the carnage. Then, in November, an agreement in faraway Dayton, Ohio, formally ended the war, allowing Sarajevans to work and play in relative safety for the first time since April 1992. But Bosnia remained divided, and even a NATO force of 60,000 could not fully guarantee the peace.

BACK IN CHAINS

Although the overall crime rate fell in 1995, the rate of *violent* crime remained frighteningly high—and the prison population kept growing. Heeding cries for longer sentences and harsher penalties, legislators passed "three strikes" laws, and wardens cut inmate privileges. In May, Alabama became the first state (followed by Arizona and Florida) to bring back chain gangs, which had been phased out, thanks to public outrage, by the 1960s. This time, only repeat offenders were put in shackles—but those with violent records were, ironically, ineligible.

Doing time . . .

Coming together in tragedy . . .

A SLAUGHTER OF INNOCENTS

Baylee Almon (left) celebrated her first birthday on April 18. The next day she was killed, along with scores of others, in the bloodiest terrorist attack in the nation's history. Authorities say right-wing militants bombed an Oklahoma City federal building, perhaps to protest the government's fiery raid on the Branch Davidian cult near Waco, Tex., exactly two years earlier. The Oklahoma bombing threw the country's political divisions into stark relief—but it united Americans in grief and anger, and prompted a deluge of aid.

11

Discovering wonders . . .

TALES FROM THE CRYPT

For seven years, Dr. Kent Weeks, an Egyptologist at Cairo's American University, had dug through tons of rubble, seeking the secrets of a tomb long believed barren. In May he announced his team's discovery: Behind a once hidden door lay the biggest mausoleum in the Valley of the Kings. The site, with at least 67 chambers, appeared to be the resting place of 50 sons of Ramses II—Egypt's grandest pharaoh (reign: 1279–1212 B.C.) and the reputed nemesis of Moses.

Holding on to love . . .

A FALLEN STAR FIGHTS BACK

In the movies, Christopher Reeve, 43, was best known for playing Superman. But his strapping body proved all too fragile in May, when a riding accident left him paralyzed from the neck down. After surviving an operation to insert a titanium rod into his spine, the actor faced a more insidious danger: despair. That's where love came in—from his wife, Dana Morosini (with him, left, at a charity dinner in November), from his three children, from fans, and from friends like Robin Williams, whose zaniness worked wonders. After the comedian visited him, disguised as a mad Russian proctologist, said Reeve, "I laughed, and I knew I was going to be all right."

15

Not forgetting . . .

WAR AND REMEMBRANCE

To those who lived through World War II, it hardly seemed possible that half a century had passed since the great conflagration ended. The anniversaries (V-E Day in May, V-J Day in August) were celebrated around the globe, with ceremonies official and unofficial, mirthful and mournful. In London, to commemorate the August 6 atomic bombing of Hiroshima, members of the Campaign for Nuclear Disarmament lighted 200 candles—approximately one for every thousand victims of the blast and radiation.

Getting the job done . . .

MONUMENT TO PERSEVERANCE
Crazy Horse—the Oglala Sioux leader who crushed Custer at Little Bighorn—was a man who never gave up. So was Korczak Ziolkowski. The sculptor (who helped carve Mount Rushmore's presidential heads) began blasting the warrior's likeness into South Dakota's Thunderhead Mountain in 1948, at the request of another Sioux chief. When Ziolkowski died in 1982, his equally persistent widow, Ruth, and several of their 10 children carried on the work. In March, drillers finished the nose and cheeks. When it's done— someday—the statue will measure 563 feet tall by 641 feet long.

Choosing sides . . .

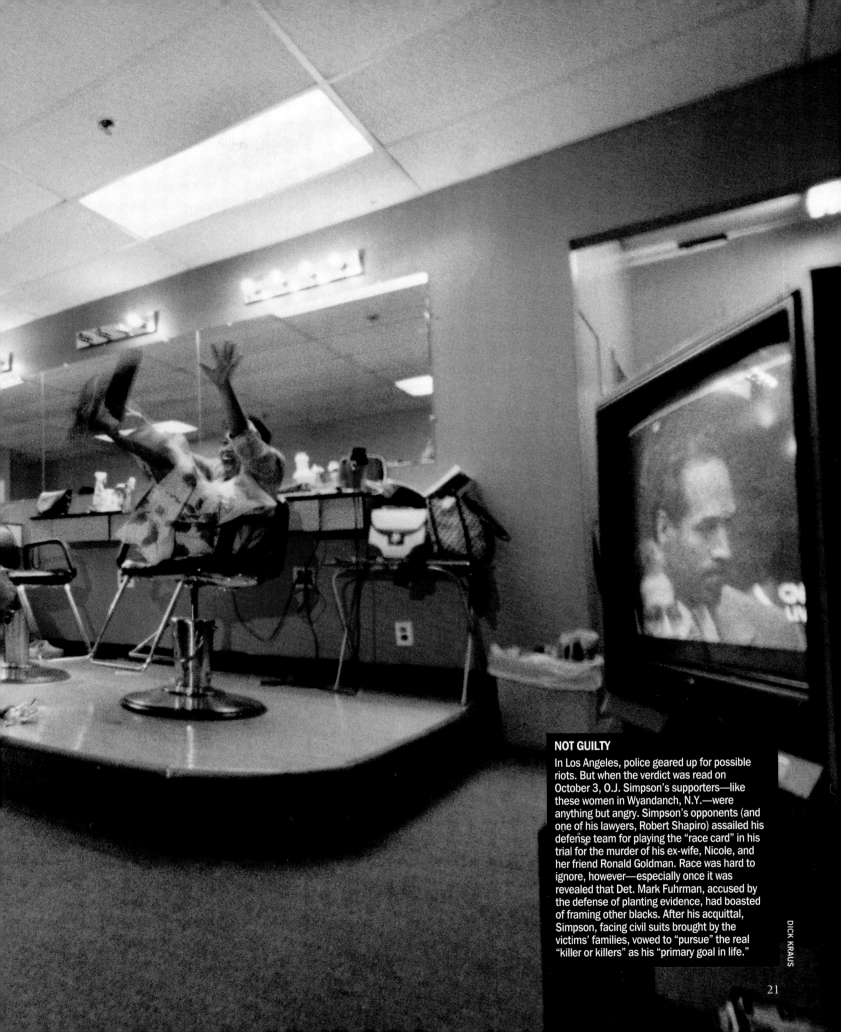

NOT GUILTY

In Los Angeles, police geared up for possible riots. But when the verdict was read on October 3, O.J. Simpson's supporters—like these women in Wyandanch, N.Y.—were anything but angry. Simpson's opponents (and one of his lawyers, Robert Shapiro) assailed his defense team for playing the "race card" in his trial for the murder of his ex-wife, Nicole, and her friend Ronald Goldman. Race was hard to ignore, however—especially once it was revealed that Det. Mark Fuhrman, accused by the defense of planting evidence, had boasted of framing other blacks. After his acquittal, Simpson, facing civil suits brought by the victims' families, vowed to "pursue" the real "killer or killers" as his "primary goal in life."

21

Working it out

FRIENDS IN NEED

It was a post–cold war conundrum. President Clinton (far left) wanted U.S. forces to join NATO peacekeepers in Bosnia, but to secure Congress's blessing he needed Boris Yeltsin to send troops too. Yeltsin needed Washington's friendship, but hard-liners at home would not let him put Russian soldiers under NATO command. In October, at Franklin D. Roosevelt's estate in Hyde Park, N.Y., the two leaders deftly got each other off the political hook: Russians would serve, they agreed, but the details would be worked out by the generals involved.

STEPHAN SAVOIA

23

Postage for **a first-class letter jumps** from 29 to 32 cents.

Convicted crack user **Marion Barry** completes a post-prison comeback, taking office for his fourth term as mayor of Washington, D.C.

Qubilah Shabazz, a daughter of **Malcolm X,** is indicted for hiring a hit man to kill Nation of Islam leader **Louis Farrakhan.** Shabazz is sentenced to two years' probation and ordered to undergo psychiatric treatment. Farrakhan thinks she was "set up" and accuses the government of trying to divide black America.

PGA champ **Arnold Palmer** launches a 24-hour cable channel devoted to golf.

Dumb and Dumber, starring **Jim Carrey** and **Jeff Daniels** as two quixotic nitwits, is the nation's No. 1 movie.

King of the Hill

The conservative revolution took Congress on January 4. For the first time since 1955, a Republican majority sat in both houses—and the halls rang with a chant of "Newt! Newt! Newt!" The new Speaker had plotted his party's rise (and his own) for a decade, sending monthly tapes of his gospel to GOP candidates nationwide. Now, in his Contract with America, Newt Gingrich had declared war on the liberal legacies of the New Deal and the Great Society. But land mines dotted the battlefield: public misgivings (polls showed most voters opposed gutting social services), veto threats—and Gingrich. Though he reigned supreme as a power broker, the family-values ideologist faced cries of hypocrisy for having dumped his ailing first wife, and ethics charges over dubious fund-raising and a fat book deal. Another challenge to his ambitions: his current spouse. "I don't want him to be President," she said, "and I don't think he should be."

DENIS PAQUIN/AP

Hillary Clinton says that she's due for an image change. Notes the First Lady: "I am surprised at the way people seem to perceive me. Sometimes I read stories and hear things about me and I go 'Ugh, I wouldn't like her either.'"

Three months after announcing a merger of their creative and commercial talents, **Steven Spielberg**, **Jeffrey Katzenberg** and **David Geffen** name their multimedia conglomerate DreamWorks SKG.

Fitness guru **Susan** ("Stop the insanity!") **Powter** files for bankruptcy.

Oprah Winfrey admits that she smoked cocaine in her youth.

A suicide bomb attack by the terrorist organization **Islamic Jihad** kills 19 people at a bus stop in Nordiya, Israel.

The Earth Roared

The material damage was awesome enough: 5,000 dead, 300,000 homeless, 50,000 buildings ruined. But the quake that rocked Kobe on January 17 also shook a nation's faith that nature must bow to technological genius. Temblor-prone Japan took pride in its strict building codes, its disaster-training programs, its earthquake-prediction research. Yet when the ground opened beneath this port city, it exposed a lode of human fallibility. Some "earthquake proof" structures, such as the Hanshin Expressway (right), toppled. Water mains snapped and fires raged unchecked. Red tape snarled rescue efforts. Luckily the quake, a 7.2 on the Richter scale, struck at 5:46 a.m., before commuters hit the roads and rails. No one looted, neighbor helped neighbor, and the yakuza (the Japanese mob) donated food and water.

NOBURO HASHIMOTO/SYGMA

"Females have biological problems staying in a ditch for 30 days because they get infections," declares **Newt Gingrich,** speaking about women in combat. "Men are little piglets. You drop them in the ditch, they roll around in it." In response to the Speaker's notion that "males are biologically driven to go out and hunt giraffes," Representative **Patricia Schroeder** points out that in all her years of working alongside men, she has yet to meet a single giraffe hunter.

The Hits, an album by country crooner **Garth Brooks,** tops the pop music charts.

New Jersey Governor **Christine Todd Whitman** becomes the first governor—and the first woman—to deliver the Republican response to a presidential State of the Union address.

People magazine names actor **Brad Pitt** the Sexiest Man Alive.

The Trial Begins

Christopher Darden was speaking for his boss Marcia Clark as well as himself when he addressed the jury on January 24: "I think it's fair to say I have the toughest job in town today." The two Los Angeles prosecutors (right) were taking on an icon—a former football hero, a star of silly movies and memorable commercials, a ghetto kid who had grown rich enough to buy the best defense team in the U.S.A. True, O.J. Simpson had plenty going against him: bloody gloves and socks, DNA evidence, a history of spousal abuse. But did he murder his ex-wife, Nicole Brown Simpson, and her friend Ronald Goldman? The defendant's chief lawyer, Johnnie Cochran, warned against a "rush to judgment." And as the televised testimony began, a rapt nation learned that there would be no rush at all.

HARRY BENSON

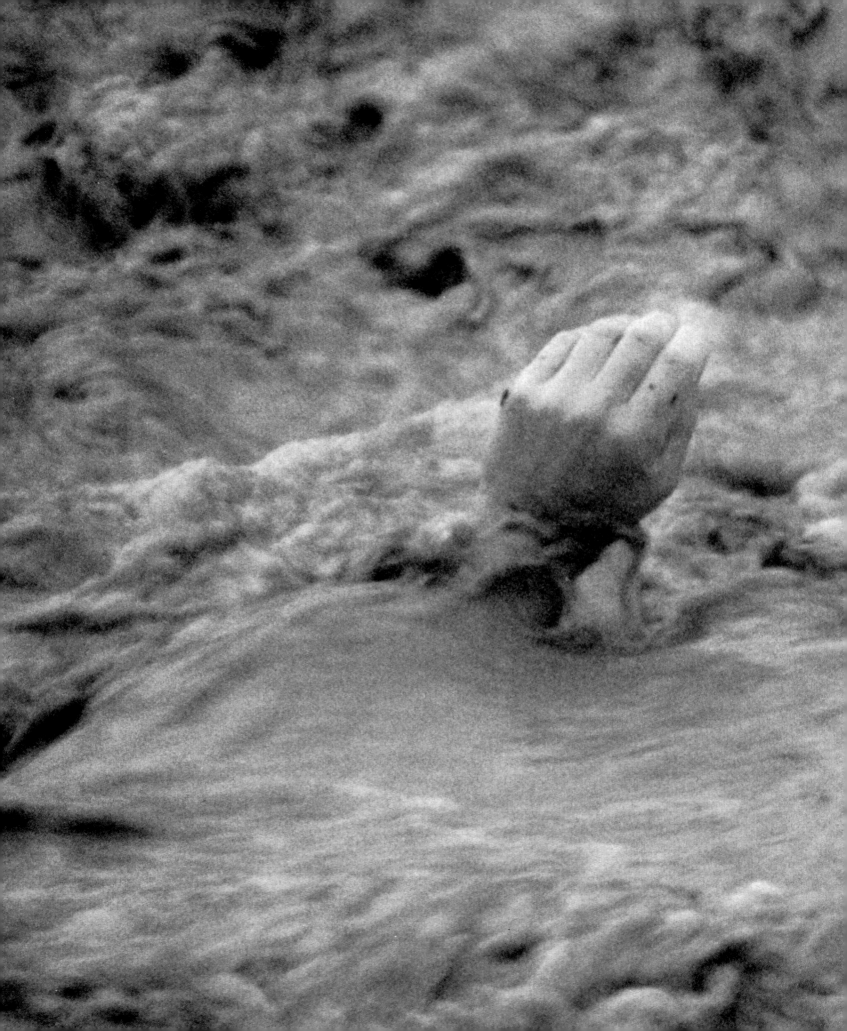

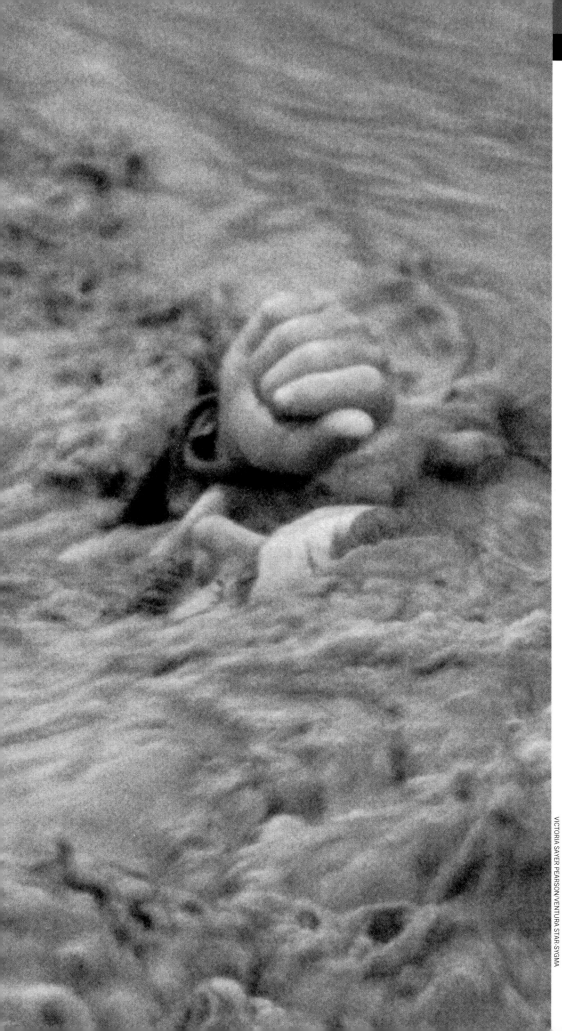

VICTORIA SAYER PEARSON/VENTURA STAR-SYGMA

Swept Away

The National Weather Service classified it as the kind of downpour that happens once in a hundred years. "This is one never-ending storm," marveled a spokesman. Torrential rain lashed California for nearly two weeks in January, laying a path of misery from Sonoma's vineyards to the canyons of Los Angeles. Floods killed 11 people and drove thousands from their homes. Furious winds uprooted redwoods from the sodden soil. In Santa Barbara, Highway 101 became a canal. And in Ventura, a homeless man (left) was waiting to be evacuated from a riverside camp when the torrent grabbed him. He was lucky: The fire department's Swift Water Rescue Team grabbed him back, and he got off with nothing more than a bad chill.

Among Hollywood's cold-eyed sharks and hot-tempered ego-trippers, he is that rarest of creatures: a nice guy. Or so the media have decreed. But even if he chafes at the Boy Scout image—"They've got to label you something," he groans—Tom Hanks has made movie-star decency bankable again. Without the benefit of big guns, awesome pecs or a love god's face, Hanks, 38, was the highest-grossing actor in the business by the start of 1995. He had chosen roles where heart, wit and character were key—and played them with breathtaking subtlety and force. In March his title turn as a wise simpleton in *Forrest Gump* won him his second Academy Award (his first was for *Philadelphia,* in which he played a courageous gay lawyer with AIDS), making Hanks the only leading man since Spencer Tracy to snag two in a row. And in June he premiered in his most demanding role yet, as astronaut Jim Lovell in *Apollo 13.* To play the part, Hanks had to master a flight simulator, learn to utter lines like "Roll CAL angle at minus two" with casual conviction, and spend long seconds floating weightless in a NASA jet nicknamed the Vomit Comet. His portrayal of a spit-and-polish spaceman was light-years away from his early slapstick roles (remember *Bosom Buddies*?) and his heartstring-pulling recent ones—but as Lovell, an unassuming hero and a consummate team player, Hanks was right at home.

TomHanks

President Clinton proposes **upping the minimum wage** from $4.25 to $5.15. Republicans claim the increase will hurt business.

The American Academy of Pediatrics recommends the distribution of **condoms in high schools** as a way to combat sexually transmitted diseases and teen pregnancy.

Myrlie Evers-Williams, widow of slain civil rights leader **Medgar Evers,** is elected chairman of the NAACP.

At a soccer match in Dublin, English fans, perturbed that their team is trailing by one goal, **attack Irish spectators.** The ensuing riot, which results in 60 wounded, puts a stop to the game.

Ben & Jerry's ice cream names Robert Holland, a management consultant, the winner of their **"Yo! I'm Your CEO"** essay contest. The new chief's favorite flavors: Cherry Garcia, Maple Walnut and White Russian.

A Sad Retreat

The United Nations sent troops to Somalia in 1992 with a modest goal: to keep warring clans from blocking food shipments to a starving people. As the U.N. force swelled to 30,000, its mission expanded to nation-building, but in this tortured land outsiders could not impose order. The numbers soon dwindled. And on February 28, the 2,400 remaining troops began their exodus, spurring renewed fighting among Somalis and looting at Mogadishu airport. (At right, a woman pleads with a Pakistani soldier to let her keep her haul.) Though U.S. Marines had withdrawn in 1994, nearly 2,000 returned—leading a multinational force of 14,000—to guard the evacuation. Trading volleys with militiamen, the Yanks exited last. Said their commander, Lt. Gen. Anthony Zinni: "I feel bad that things did not work out."

SCOTT PETERSON/GAMMA LIAISON

Foul Ball

When spring training began in February, it looked as if the strike would never end. Even President Clinton struck out when he tried to get the team owners and the talent to play ball. As replacement players bumbled through exhibition games in Florida and Arizona, fans mainly stayed away; at a Dodger game (left), some diehards brought along inflatable friends to fill a few empty seats. In April, however, just as it seemed the national pastime would go the way of doorstep milk delivery, both sides agreed to a time-out— and baseball was back. The eight-month dispute had brought no new deal between the millionaire workers and their billionaire bosses. "I think we've both proven how strong we are," said Colorado Rockies owner Jerry McMorris. "But I think we've severely damaged our game."

With her new single "Take a Bow" topping the charts, **Madonna** does just that—when she surpasses **Whitney Houston** as the female solo artist with the most No. 1 pop hits. The new record: 11.

The blue-suited workers of IBM have the option of loosening their ties and even pulling on their blue jeans, now that the computer giant has officially relaxed its **dress code** to include "business casual."

Concluding that tobacco companies knowingly withheld the fact that nicotine is addictive, a federal judge rules that **"nicotine-dependent persons"** have standing to seek punitive damages in a class action lawsuit.

"We are as nervous as cats," confesses **Bill Clinton** before teeing off with **Gerald Ford** and **George Bush** at a charity golf tournament. Before the 18 holes are finished, the team has injured three people, including an elderly woman whose nose is bloodied by a Bush ball gone awry.

A City's Agony

The name Grozny means "terrible," reflecting the Chechen capital's age-old reputation as a hotbed of fierce rebels and bandits. But nothing could be as terrible as the rain of Russian bombs that pounded the separatist bastion in the first weeks of 1995. Most of Grozny's 400,000 residents fled, leaving guerrillas and a few civilians—mainly ethnic Russians with no relatives to run to in nearby villages. By early February, when the tanks broke through (top left) and President Dzhokhar Dudayev, who had declared Chechnya independent in 1991, went into hiding, the city lay in ruins. Still, Moscow's forces had taken heavy losses too, and skirmishes continued. In July—after rebels seized hostages at a hospital in Russia, sparking a bloody shoot-out—the two sides, exhausted, signed a truce.

JEREMY NICHOLL/MATRIX(4)

GregLouganis

Until February 1995 it was possible to see him as a man blessed by the gods. The first male diver to win double golds at consecutive Olympic Games, Greg Louganis was one of America's best-loved athletes—humble, handsome and serene, or so we thought. Then, on *20/20,* Louganis, 35, revealed that he had AIDS. (He had announced that he was gay the previous June.) He had known he was infected, he said, since early 1988; what's more, he had kept it secret from Olympic officials even after gashing his head during a preliminary dive at the Seoul Games. Although medical experts insisted that chlorine and dilution would have eliminated any danger to other divers, Louganis's confession created a furor. But when he published his autobiography in March, censure turned to sympathy. Abandoned at birth by his parents, he had been terrorized by his alcoholic adoptive father; schoolmates had tormented him for his dark skin (his biological father was Samoan), his stutter and his "sissyish" devotion to acrobatics. He had survived three suicide attempts and a long string of abusive relationships. "I want people to know who I am and what I went through," Louganis wrote in *Breaking the Surface.* "I wouldn't wish my life on anyone."

Tony Bennett, 68 and extremely popular with the Generation X crowd, snags the album of the year Grammy for his *MTV Unplugged.* Other winners: **Bruce Springsteen,** four Grammys, including best song, for "Streets of Philadelphia"; **Sheryl Crow,** three awards (best record, new artist and female pop vocal) for "All I Wanna Do"; **Melissa Etheridge,** best female rock vocal for "Come to My Window"; **Queen Latifah,** best rap solo for "U.N.I.T.Y."; **Salt-N-Pepa,** best rap group for "None of Your Business"; and **Johnny Cash,** best contemporary folk album for *American Recordings.*

Endeavour blasts off on March 2, embarking on the longest flight in U.S. space shuttle history: 16 days.

Quickly fulfilling a campaign promise, New York's new governor, Republican **George Pataki,** reinstates the death penalty after 18 years, making his the 38th state with capital punishment.

Riding High

For 12 days in March and April, Hillary and Chelsea Clinton immersed themselves in the exotic glories and epic miseries of South Asia. The journey—which took the pair from village squares to the Taj Mahal to a ride on Nepal's transit system (right)—was an intergenerational learning experience. It was also an opportunity for reputation polishing. The First Lady had been panned for her roles in the Whitewater scandal and the health-care-reform debacle; now she won raves as an ambassador for women's and children's issues. And the First Daughter, who had long been shielded from public scrutiny, stepped into the limelight—newly liberated from her braces and her adolescent awkwardness. The 15-year-old's blond tresses impressed her Indian peers, and her brains wowed Benazir Bhutto. "We found Chelsea very knowledgeable on Islamic issues," said Pakistan's prime minister.

JOHN GAPS III/AP

A Repentant Racist

A measure of the distance American race relations have come in three decades: former Alabama governor George C. Wallace—whose motto had been Segregation Forever—holding hands with civil rights activists at a Montgomery church. The occasion was the 30th anniversary of a march from Selma to Montgomery led by Martin Luther King Jr., a protest Wallace had opposed so vehemently that President Johnson sent troops to protect the peaceful demonstrators. But since being crippled by a would-be assassin in 1972, Wallace had changed his ways. Now 75 and too feeble to address the crowd himself, he spoke through an aide: "May your lessons never be forgotten." Indeed, with affirmative action and antipoverty programs under attack, rights advocates feared their gains were slipping away. Said NAACP chairman Myrlie Evers-Williams: "The struggle continues."

To the horror (or relief) of many dieters, scientists at Rockefeller University report that **every person has a set body weight** to which his or her metabolism naturally gravitates.

Gerry Adams, leader of Sinn Fein, the political wing of the **Irish Republican Army,** holds two fund-raisers in New York City and pays a St. Patrick's Day visit to the White House. Until last year's IRA cease-fire, the U.S. had forbidden official contact with Sinn Fein, condemning it as a terrorist organization.

Jerry Lewis, the American comedian adored by the French, makes his Broadway debut at age 69, playing the devil in *Damn Yankees.*

The FDA approves Varivax, America's first **chicken pox** vaccine.

The Brady Bunch Movie, which shows the 1970s TV clan grooving happily in the 1990s (though still partial to polyester), is No. 1 at the box office.

No Refuge

A year after Hutu extremists murdered half a million Tutsi in Rwanda, the tables were turned. Now it was Tutsi-led rebels who held power and Hutu refugees who filled camps on both sides of the country's borders. New troubles struck the Hutu in March, this time in neighboring Burundi (whose ethnic makeup matches Rwanda's: 85 percent Hutu, 15 percent Tutsi). After a Hutu government minister was shot and a Tutsi politician was crucified and gutted, Tutsi militias went on an ethnic cleansing campaign in the Burundian capital, Bujumbura, and in a camp for Rwandan refugees. Thousands of Rwandan Hutu (right) now had to flee Burundi for Tanzania. Meanwhile, in Rwanda, the new regime was urging its Hutu citizens to go back to their homes. But fears of vengeance from bitter Tutsi—and threats by Hutu hard-liners against anyone who cooperated with the government—kept most from returning. In April chaos erupted as Rwandan troops sought to empty the country's biggest refugee camp. When the smoke cleared, 2,000 Hutu lay dead.

A sarin nerve gas attack on Tokyo's subway system during the morning rush hour of March 20 kills 12 and injures 5,500. Two days later, police seize two tons of sarin-producing chemicals from the offices of the apocalyptic cult **Aum Shinrikyo**. The sect denies involvement, but its leader, a partially blind yogi named **Shoko Asahara**, has gone into hiding.

Queen Elizabeth visits South Africa for the first time since 1947.

Convicted rapist and former heavyweight champion **Mike Tyson** is released on good behavior after serving three years of a six-year prison sentence.

Tejano singer **Selena** is fatally shot on March 31 in Corpus Christi, Tex., by **Yolanda Saldivar**, the former president of her fan club. Saldivar is apprehended after a 10-hour standoff, during which she locks herself in a pickup truck and holds a gun to her head.

The Second Coming

One good thing came out of the baseball strike: In March, basketball got back its Michelangelo. Michael Jordan had retired in 1993, after leading the Chicago Bulls to three straight NBA championships. Believing his sport held no more challenges, he had turned to baseball. But his record with the Chicago White Sox Double A team, the Birmingham Barons, was mediocre—and during spring training, loath to cross picket lines, he set his bat aside. When Jordan, 32, showed up for practice with the Bulls, companies where he had endorsement deals saw their stocks rise. And when he released a statement reading simply "I'm back," fans who heard the news on Beijing loudspeakers cheered. After wobbling through a few games wearing his baseball number, 45, Jordan reclaimed his old jersey—No. 23—and began to regain his legendary form. The Bulls stood by their man, despite a $100,000 NBA fine for allowing the unauthorized switch.

ROBERT KOZLOFF/AP

Pulp Fiction's Uma Thurman stepped out with her dad.

A slim Oprah Winfrey—train in tow—impressed the starry crowd.

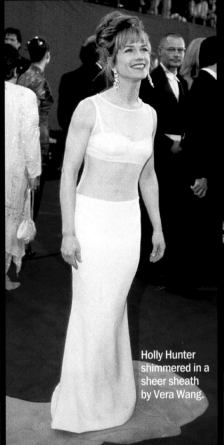

Holly Hunter shimmered in a sheer sheath by Vera Wang.

Jessica Lange was superfine in a lacy Calvin Klein.

First-time host David Letterman crashed and burned, but the stars sparkled— often literally—throughout the ceremony (running time: 3:35) and the post-show soirees. They had to: In Hollywood, all nights lead to . . .

Oscar Night

Susan Sarandon and Tim Robbins kept their politics off the podium.

Best Actor nominee John Travolta and wife Kelly Preston

Tom Hanks, with wife Rita Wilson, chose the tieless tux look.

Courtney Love partied with date Amanda de Cadenet.

While others squeezed it in, Andie MacDowell played it loose.

Jodie Foster wore Armani, her favorite designer.

And the winner is...

■ PICTURE—*FORREST GUMP* ■ DIRECTOR—ROBERT ZEMECKIS, *FORREST GUMP* ■ ACTOR—TOM HANKS, *FORREST GUMP* ■ ACTRESS—JESSICA LANGE, *BLUE SKY* ■ SUPPORTING ACTOR—MARTIN LANDAU, *ED WOOD* ■ SUPPORTING ACTRESS—DIANNE WIEST, *BULLETS OVER BROADWAY* ■ ORIGINAL SCREENPLAY—QUENTIN TARANTINO, ROGER AVARY, *PULP FICTION* ■ SCREENPLAY ADAPTATION—ERIC ROTH, *FORREST GUMP* ■ ORIGINAL SONG—"CAN YOU FEEL THE LOVE TONIGHT," *THE LION KING* ■ FOREIGN LANGUAGE FILM—*BURNT BY THE SUN* (RUSSIA).

Madonna strikes a pose with brother Chris Ciccone.

Quentin Tarantino's Best Director chances were as slim as his tie.

"I was looking for an American symbol," said Amex-clad Aussie Lizzy Gardiner, who shared Costume Design honors for *The Adventures of Priscilla, Queen of the Desert.*

The **University of Connecticut women's basketball team,** the Huskies, beats the University of Tennessee Lady Vols, 70–64, to capture their first NCAA championship—making them only the second women's tournament winner to finish a season undefeated.

Fourteen years after joining the Supreme Court, its first female justice, **Sandra Day O'Connor,** becomes the first woman to assume the duties of acting chief justice when the real chief (**William Rehnquist**) and his deputy (**John Paul Stevens**) are out of town for a day.

New York City kicks the habit on April 10 when it enacts **a ban on cigarette smoking** in most public places, including restaurants, hotels and even outdoor stadiums.

Terror in the Heartland

When a massive truck-bomb exploded in Oklahoma City on the morning of April 19, a reeling nation blamed foreign terrorists. The blast at the Alfred P. Murrah Federal Building killed 169 people—including more than a dozen children in a day-care center. Surely, Americans did not do such things to one another. But after the arrest of a gulf war vet named Timothy McVeigh, the national soul-searching began. The spotlight fell on the rising militia movement: an armed, Internet-surfing underground whose members styled themselves patriots. Some of their notions were easy to dismiss— they preached that U.N. troops in black helicopters were coming to implant citizens with microchips—but their core ideas were not. Love of guns combined with hatred of big government had become a mainstream credo, from radio airwaves to the halls of Congress. Were talk jocks and politicians partly responsible for the bombing? Their answer: Of course not.

President **Bill Clinton** and Vice President **Al Gore** release their 1994 tax returns. Gore (income: $411,713) made more than his boss ($263,900). The First Couple itemized and paid $55,313 in federal taxes; the Second Couple, who opted for the $6,350 standard deduction, paid $142,688.

A University of Chicago study reports that **married people are happier**, healthier and more financially stable than those who live with a romantic partner or are single.

New York Sen. **Alfonse D'Amato** offers a rare apology on the Senate floor after he mocks **Lance Ito**, the judge for the O.J. Simpson trial, on **Don Imus's** radio show. The Republican legislator had feigned a Japanese accent and referred to the Japanese American jurist as "little Judge Ito."

John Grisham's *The Rainmaker* tops the *New York Times* best-seller list.

Digging and Praying

The Oklahoma City bombing wrought its devastation in an instant, but it took 46 days to retrieve the victims from the rubble. The survivors all emerged within the first 10 hours. A few, like the man at top left, walked away from the Murrah Building under their own power. Others were extricated from tons of concrete. Among them was Dana Bradley, 20 (top right); to free her, doctors had to amputate a leg on the spot. Rescuers came from around the country. Like Miamian Skip Fernandez and his helper, Aspen (bottom left), they worked past the point of exhaustion, under perilous conditions. Many went for weeks without seeing their families. (At bottom right, bomb-disposal expert Rocky Yardley has a rare visit with son Max.) The daily display of heroism mitigated some of the horror, as did an outpouring of aid. The city was inundated with food, clothing and medical supplies— as well as 600 teddy bears, sent to comfort bereaved families.

Kansas City Chiefs quarterback **Joe Montana,** widely considered to be the greatest in the game, retires from football. During a press conference in San Francisco—where he had played 14 out of his 16 pro seasons and led the 49ers to four Super Bowl wins—the 38-year-old athlete explains his decision: "It felt like a job."

Three hundred people are hospitalized by gas fumes that spread through a railroad station in the Japanese city of Yokohama. As they did with the sarin gas attack in the Tokyo subway system in March, police suspect the cult **Aum Shinrikyo,** which again denies involvement.

The Centers for Disease Control and Prevention reports that the suicide rate among children ages 10 to 14 increased 120 percent between 1980 and 1992. The most dramatic changes were among black males (300 percent) and white females (233 percent).

A Warrior Atones

Saigon fell in April 1975, but on the battlegrounds of American opinion the Vietnam war has never ended. So when the conflict's chief U.S. architect observed the 20th anniversary with a mea culpa, he sparked a political firestorm. "We were wrong, terribly wrong," wrote Robert S. McNamara, 78, in his memoir, *In Retrospect: The Tragedy & Lessons of Vietnam.* Though the former Secretary of Defense (under JFK and LBJ) wept during a book-tour interview, critics were unmoved— they rejected his confession as incomplete and absurdly tardy. In Vietnam, however, the book went over well. (The government said it "squares with reality.") And in November, four months after their countries resumed full diplomatic ties, two old antagonists met in Hanoi. The war, McNamara told reporters after shaking hands with General Vo Nguyen Giap, 84, was "a tragedy for both nations. There's really no difference between him and me."

Writer **Aleksandr Solzhenitsyn,** 76, the anti-Soviet dissident, who during his 20-year exile lived in Vermont and routinely disparaged Western materialism and pop culture, stars as the host of a *Charlie Rose*-like talk show back home in Russia.

The Unabomber—so dubbed by the FBI because his initial bomb targets were universities and airlines—strikes again, on April 24, for the 16th time since 1978. **Gilbert Murray,** the chief lobbyist for the California Forestry Association, dies after opening a mail bomb at the organization's Sacramento office.

Baseball season opens three weeks late on April 25, when the Los Angeles Dodgers defeat the Florida Marlins 8–7 in Miami. Still angered by the strike, many fans stay home, and those in the stadium greet both teams with boos.

A Case for Solomon

Neighbors cried "monster" as Otakar Kirchner lifted Danny Warburton—known to the world by his court-ordained pseudonym, Baby Richard—from the arms of his adoptive parents. Illinois suburbanites Kim and Robert Warburton (far right) had raised the four-year-old since infancy, and their fight to keep him had roused wide support. But Danny's biological parents had a strong claim too. His mother, Daniela, gave him up at birth because she thought her fiancé had left her. Otakar eventually called, but she told him their baby was dead. Only when the couple reconciled—just after the state's 30-day limit for contesting an adoption had passed—did he learn the truth. The legal struggle ended in April when the Supreme Court refused the case. "I don't want to," Danny wailed as he was carried off. Within weeks he was calling the Kirchners Mommy and Daddy— but would scars linger? No one could say.

The Hip & The Hot

In 1995 we connected: In film, fashion and on TV, men and women gamely shared clothing and accessories (makeup, stogies). In cyberspace, Peorians partied with Parisians. And in the clubs, we found a clean, though not necessarily clean-cut, way to dance . . .

And also...

◼ Melatonin, the best-selling hormone believed to ease insomnia and jet lag—and to slow aging

◼ Faux leopard-skin garb

◼ Coffee bars: The leader of the pack, Starbucks, had 17 cafés when it opened in 1987. In 1995 there were 709 Starbucks nationwide and hundreds of imitators (many in superstore bookshops) serving up countless cups of espresso, cappuccino and iced latte.

◼ Clunky-heeled shoes (see Lisa Kudrow's feet, far left)

BEST OF *FRIENDS*
The year's hottest sitcom spawned equally hot spin-offs: the "Rachel" haircut (see Jennifer Aniston, center); a hit single (the show's theme song, "I'll Be There for You," by the Rembrandts); and endless groups of gorgeous 20-and-30-somethings (like Kudrow, Aniston and their castmates, from left, David Schwimmer, Matt LeBlanc, Courteney Cox and Matthew Perry) hanging out in copycat ads and TV shows.

TRESSED FOR SUCCESS: "Less is more" was the prevailing rule for men's hair. Some opted for a raggedly clipped crew cut (from left, the once luxuriantly maned Brad Pitt, as well as Keanu Reeves and Jim Carrey). Others chose the Caesar (as in Julius) variation, worn by George Clooney (near left), a star of the year's hottest TV drama, *ER.*

STOGIES Bans on smoking aside, cigars were an equal opportunity pastime at upscale restaurants and clubs.

FOAM DANCING For the Safer Sex '90s, frolicking in foam (actually soapsuds) was an exotic, but not overly erotic, pleasure.

CYBERCAFES At these digitally equipped eateries, caffeinated Internet fans networked—with each other and pals far away.

DRAG QUEENS Cross-dressing was hip on Broadway (*Victor/Victoria*) and on screen, where Wesley Snipes vamped in *To Wong Fu* . . .

BLACK AND BROWN Dark chic (jet-black and cocoa-brown lipstick and nail polish) was the makeup of the moment among teenage mall rats, models, businesswomen—and for macho movie star Antonio (*Desperado*) Banderas.

The FBI makes a second arrest in the Oklahoma City bombing case. **Terry Nichols,** an Army friend of prime suspect **Timothy McVeigh,** is charged with aiding in the attack and participating in the "malicious damage of a federal building."

Former President **George Bush** turns in his lifetime membership to the **National Rifle Association,** citing a fund-raising letter that, Bush says, "deeply offends my own sense of decency and honor." The NRA missive had described federal agents as "jackbooted thugs" who terrorize American citizens.

Dow Corning, the country's leading maker of silicone breast implants, files for bankruptcy. The company cites the numerous lawsuits brought against it by women claiming health problems due to the implants.

Toasting a Triumph

From a balcony at Buckingham Palace, the Queen Mother waved to a roaring throng—just as she had done half a century earlier. In Hyde Park, thousands jitterbugged for joy. And in the skies over London (right), the RAF put on a smashing show. It was May 8, the 50th anniversary of the end of World War II in Europe, and the whole continent was celebrating. But the dozens of world leaders who attended Britain's opening festivities two days earlier had already moved on. They started V-E Day in Paris, where outgoing French President François Mitterrand lit a flame at the Tomb of the Unknown Soldier; then they flew to Berlin, the onetime Nazi capital, for more pomp and speeches. On May 9, President Clinton joined the group in Moscow. "You wrote some of the greatest chapters in the history of heroism," Clinton told the Russians—but to protest their current war in Chechnya, he and most of the other visiting dignitaries sat out a military parade.

RICHARD COOKE

Short of amending the U.S. Constitution, lawmakers and voters cannot impose **term limits** on members of Congress, says a 5–4 ruling by the Supreme Court.

New Zealand's *Black Magic 1* defeats the United States' *Stars & Stripes* (led by past champ **Dennis Conner**) to win the **America's Cup.** Though the U.S. lost the race, it did earn a place in America's Cup history: Another competitor, *America³*, was the first yacht to be sailed by an all-female crew.

Dallas elects **Ron Kirk,** an attorney and former Texas secretary of state, as its mayor. He is the first African American to lead a major Texas city.

Connie Chung is fired from the *CBS Evening News* after reported run-ins with her coanchor of two years, **Dan Rather.**

A Bloody Plague

In the early months of 1995, tales of epidemics were all the rage. *Outbreak* was a top-grossing movie, *Robin Cook's Virus* was a hit TV film, *The Coming Plague* and *The Hot Zone* were popular reads. Then, in Kikwit, Zaire (right), microbial mayhem struck. The pestilence was first reported at the city hospital, where it attacked those who came into unprotected contact with victims or their bodily fluids. The symptoms were horrific—sufferers bled from every orifice as their internal organs liquefied. The culprit, identified in May by the U.S. Centers for Disease Control and Prevention: Ebola, an untreatable virus discovered in 1976 when it erupted in Zaire and Sudan. By the time this year's outbreak ended in August, 244 of the 315 victims were dead. Scientists explain that the recent upsurge in once exotic ailments, from AIDS to hantavirus, is largely humanity's doing. As we have colonized rain forests, changed our sexual behavior and flown around the globe, germs have gained new footholds. The war against infectious disease—believed nearly over just a few decades ago—is clearly far from won.

La Victoire!

Twice before, he had run for president of France, and twice he had lost. But in May, Paris Mayor Jacques Chirac (on balcony), 62, became the country's first conservative helmsman since 1981. His victory over Lionel Jospin owed much to a 12 percent unemployment rate and much to voters' restlessness: After 14 years under Socialist François Mitterrand, the French craved change. But perhaps the crucial factor in Chirac's success was his daughter Claude, 32, who acted as his image consultant. Before she stepped in, the former prime minister had a stodgy, stiff-backed persona; his nickname was *Le Bulldozer.* Claude got her father to dress more casually, lighten his demeanor, even share a stage with Madonna—and when he won, young Parisians partied in the streets. The cheering faded quickly, however. Chirac soon faced an international uproar over his revival of nuclear testing, strikes and riots over his austerity program, and a campaign of terrorist bombings to protest France's ties to civil war–torn Algeria.

Citing security concerns, the Secret Service closes the White House stretch of Pennsylvania Avenue to traffic indefinitely. Three days later a gun-toting man jumps the South Lawn fence. The intruder, **Leland Modjeski,** 37, a former doctoral student, is shot and wounded. It is the third major breach of White House security in nine months. In the fall of 1994, a truck driver named **Frank Corder,** 38, had crashed a small plane on the grounds. The Cessna 150 then skidded into a wall beneath the President's bedroom. Corder died upon impact. Six weeks later **Francisco Duran,** 26, a dishonorably discharged Army medic, fired an assault rifle at the building. (Duran is sentenced in June to 40 years in prison.) **President Clinton,** who was at home during two of the attacks, was never harmed.

On May 28, one of the worst earthquakes in Russia's history (measuring 7.5 on the Richter scale) kills more than 2,000 people when it hits **Sakhalin,** an oil-rich east-coast island in the Sea of Okhotsk.

Crash Course

In his seven other starts at the Indianapolis 500, Stan Fox had never finished better than 11th place. But at this May's Indy he made an impression millions of spectators will never forget. It happened on the very first turn: Fox's car veered to the right, brushing a rival's. Both vehicles skidded into the wall—and Fox's went airborne, disintegrating as it flew. For a terrifying moment, the driver's legs could be seen dangling like a rag doll's. And then he fell to earth, still strapped into the cockpit. Monaco's Jacques Villeneuve went on to win the race, but Fox, 42, scored a victory too: He survived his massive head injuries. After five days in a coma and 10 weeks in rehabilitation, he went home to Wisconsin with a clean bill of health.

Madam-to-the-stars **Heidi Fleiss,** 29, convicted of procuring prostitutes, is sentenced to three years in a California jail. None of her clients (among them actor **Charlie Sheen**) was charged with wrongdoing.

Bill Gates's Microsoft abandons its planned $2 billion purchase of **Intuit,** the computer software giant. The Justice Department claimed the sale would violate antitrust laws.

Senate Majority Leader **Bob Dole** denounces the entertainment industry for its sexually explicit and violent films and music. "Nightmares of depravity," he calls them. The presidential hopeful singles out media conglomerate **Time Warner** (LIFE's parent company) as a producer of violent movies (True Romance, Natural Born Killers) and music, such as the gangsta rap of **2 Live Crew.** Says director **Oliver Stone:** "It's the height of hypocrisy for Senator Dole, who wants to repeal the assault weapons ban, to blame Hollywood for the violence in our society."

Die Hard With a Vengeance, the third installment in the **Bruce Willis** series, leads the box office in its opening week.

O f all the bizarre milestones in Michael Jackson's life, one of the most shocking was his completion, in May, of a year of matrimony. The singer's marriage to Lisa Marie Presley, then 26, had come just after he settled a molestation suit (for a reported $15 to $20 million) involving a 12-year-old boy. Pundits had branded the nuptials a sham—an attempt to make the surgically feminized and cosmetically whitened Jackson, 35, look like a regular guy. They'd given the union a few months, tops. But who better to wed the biggest pop star since Elvis than Elvis's daughter? The couple marked their anniversary by smooching for LIFE, then went on TV to tell their side of the story. The child-sex charges were "lies, lies, lies," said he. Doubters of her love, said she, could "eat it." Still, trouble wouldn't stay away: A song on Jackson's comeback album, *HIStory: Past, Present, Future—Book 1,* was blasted as anti-Semitic; chagrined, he recorded an edited version. And despite two outrageous videos—one starring the newlyweds semi-nude, the other featuring a giant Jackson statue and goose-stepping troops—the double CD proved a commercial dud.

Michael**Jackson**

Lisa Marie**Presley-Jackson**

Andrew Lloyd Webber's *Sunset Boulevard* sweeps the Tony Awards with seven wins, including best musical, actress (**Glenn Close**), original score and book of a musical. Other winners: **Terrence McNally's** *Love! Valour! Compassion!,* best play; *The Heiress,* best play revival; *Show Boat,* best musical revival; **Matthew Broderick,** best actor in a musical *(How to Succeed in Business Without Really Trying);* and **Ralph Fiennes,** best actor in a play *(Hamlet).*

President Clinton issues his first veto, striking down legislation that would have cut $16.4 billion from the federal budget, including hefty chunks from education and job training programs. A revised bill is passed on July 27.

Cracked Rear View, the debut record from the roots-rock group **Hootie & the Blowfish,** is the top pop album.

A Survivor Comes Home

America was officially neutral in Bosnia's civil war. But that didn't stop a Bosnian Serb missile from cutting Scott O'Grady's plane in half on June 2 as he patrolled a NATO no-fly zone. The missile was just the first of the Air Force captain's problems. After ejecting from his F-16, O'Grady, 29, parachuted into a forest full of hostile Serb fighters. For six days and nights he hid out, living on ants, leaves and rainwater and praying that the guerrillas beating the bushes would miss his thicket. NATO marshaled its reconnaissance jets and spy satellites; finally, the searchers made radio contact. And as dawn broke, 41 Marines in two Sea Stallion helicopters swooped down and whisked O'Grady away under heavy fire. Given a hero's welcome, the airman shifted credit to his rescuers: "All I was, was a scared little bunny rabbit trying to survive." Still, the book deals, movie offers and marriage proposals poured in. In a dirty, fratricidal and seemingly endless war, O'Grady's escape was the only unsullied victory yet.

At the request of prosecutor **Christopher Darden, O.J. Simpson** tries on a pair of bloody gloves, one of which, police claim, was found at the murder site, the other at Simpson's estate. The defendant manages to wriggle into the seemingly too snug Isotoners, but his struggle throws the prosecution. Though their witness explains that moisture shrank the gloves, defense attorney **Alan Dershowitz** gleefully notes: "It's Cinderella. They tried to shove a slipper on a foot, and it didn't fit."

The Houston Rockets, led by **Hakeem Olajuwon,** defeat the Orlando Magic, led by **Shaquille O'Neal,** 113–101 to win their second straight **NBA championship.** On the hockey front, the New Jersey Devils beat the Detroit Red Wings in a four-game sweep to win their first **Stanley Cup.**

The three-piece white suit that outfitted **John Travolta** in the 1977 disco classic *Saturday Night Fever* fetches $145,500 at Christie's and sets, as the auctioneer put it, "a record for polyester."

Myth America

She made her cartoon debut in June, on four 80-foot-high screens in Manhattan's Central Park. But the figure towering above an audience of 100,000 (winners of a nationwide lottery) was larger than life in more ways than one. Contrary to legend, the real Pocahontas never had a romance with Captain John Smith, nor is it likely that she saved the 17th century colonist from death at the hands of her fellow Powhatans. Fantasy, however, is what a Disney animated film is all about—and *Pocahontas* offered it in gobs. The heroine's features were partly based on those of supermodels Kate Moss and Naomi Campbell. Cuddly animals pranced through the woods trilling show tunes. Still, this movie's story line was a little grittier than, for instance, *The Little Mermaid*'s. Said Native American activist Russell Means, who supplied the voice of Pocahontas's father: "It tells the real reason why the settlers came here— to rob and pillage and kill Indians."

PIERRE ADENIS/SIPA PRESS

Politicians overtake the American Booksellers Association convention in Chicago, where **Hillary Clinton**, Gen. **Colin Powell**, Sen. **Paul Simon** (D-Ill.) and Rep. **Newt Gingrich** (R-Ga.) all hawk books. Ostensibly there to promote two tomes of his political theory, the House speaker receives more attention for his steamy novel, *1945,* featuring an alluring German dominatrix named Erika von Strasse.

A meeting set up by the Clinton administration to improve its relations with the gay community gets off to a shaky start when guests are met by **Secret Service officers wearing rubber gloves** for "protection." The White House immediately apologizes.

Batman Forever— featuring **Val Kilmer** as the caped crusader, **Jim Carrey** as the Riddler, **Tommy Lee Jones** as Two-Face, **Chris O'Donnell** as Robin and **Nicole Kidman** as Batman's love interest—makes box office history when it draws $18 million on its opening night. Also in June: the film version of Robert James Waller's best-selling romance novel, *The Bridges of Madison County,* starring **Meryl Streep** and **Clint Eastwood**.

It's a Wrap

Christo and his partner-wife Jeanne-Claude insist their art has no fixed meaning. The New York–based pair have wrapped Florida islands and Paris's Pont Neuf; their oeuvre, says Christo, is "absolutely irrational." Yet in June, when they led a crew of 210—including 90 rock climbers—in the draping of Berlin's Reichstag, the project was widely seen as a symbol of Germany's post-cold-war rebirth. Indeed, the 101-year-old structure (built to house the Kaiser's Parliament, then burned by the Nazis, bombed by the Allies and left empty by East Berlin's Communists) is entering a new era: By decade's end, it will shelter Parliament once more. It took seven days to cocoon the landmark in a million square feet of polypropylene cloth, which stayed up for two weeks, drew five million visitors and launched a citywide fad: In shopwindows and on billboards, everything from beer to shampoo was displayed under wraps.

Love

First, American heiress Marie-Chantal Miller, 26, married a prince, Pavlos of Greece, 28 (above). Then her sister, Alexand wed an Austrian one: Alexandre Egon von und zu Furstenberg.

Baywatch Uber-babe Pamela Anderson, 27, dated Mötley Crüe drummer Tommy Lee, 32, for six whole days before marrying him on a Cancún beach in February. The bride wore a white bikini; the groom, cutoffs.

Melanie Griffith, 38, split with husband Don Johnson (again) and began a very hot (and very smoochy) fling with 35-year-old Spanish heartthrob Antonio Banderas.

78

& Marriage

Also wed . . . ■ *NYPD Blue*'s Dennis Franz, 50, and Joanie Zeck, 47 ■ Princess Stephanie of Monaco, 30, and Daniel Ducruet, 31, father of her two children ■ Actor-comedian (and Roseanne ex) Tom Arnold, 36, and Julie Champnella, 22 ■ Actors Nicolas Cage, 31, and Patricia Arquette, 27 ■ Comic Martin Lawrence, 29, and Patricia Southall (a former Miss Virginia), 24

■ On Valentine's Day, a two-months-pregnant Roseanne, 42, wore red velvet (by Richard Tyler) for her third wedding—to Ben Thomas, 28, her former bodyguard.

■ Chynna Phillips, 27, was given away by her Mama and Papa (Michelle and John), and groom Billy Baldwin, 32, was toasted by his hunky brothers—Alec, Stephen and Daniel.

■ Skater Nancy Kerrigan, 25, wears designer Vera Wang on the ice but chose a mock-Wang gown for her September wedding to her agent, Jerry Solomon, 41.

■ Riccardo Mazzucchelli, 52, waited four years for his love, Ivana Trump, 46 (topped by a Thierry Mugler veil she helped design), to join him in signing on the prenuptial dotted line.

■ Actors Ted Danson, 47, and Mary Steenburgen, 42, exchanged vows in October on Martha's Vineyard. Among the guests: Bill and Hillary Clinton, Arkansas pals of the bride's.

■ Tony Randall, 75, wed actress Heather Harlan, 25, at New York's City Hall in November. Said the bride: "I'm so old-fashioned I married a man three times my age."

After 92 days of testimony, 58 witnesses, 10 dismissed jurors and 488 pieces of physical evidence, the prosecution in the **O.J. Simpson trial** rests on July 6. Total cost to L.A. County taxpayers so far: $6.47 million.

When the U.S. shuttle *Atlantis* and the Russian station *Mir* made the first post-cold-war rendezvous in space on June 29, U.S. astronaut **Norman Thagard,** who had been a guest on *Mir,* caught a ride home. After landing at Cape Canaveral on July 7, the 51-year-old physician walks off the craft. His two Soviet colleagues are carried off on stretchers. Thagard's 115 days in space is an American record.

American **Pete Sampras** defeats German **Boris Becker** in four sets to win **Wimbledon** for the third time. Top-seeded **Steffi Graf** of Germany snags her sixth title when she beats Spain's **Arantxa Sanchez Vicario** in three sets.

Panic in Paris

As such devices go, it was nothing fancy—but on a crowded commuter train, six pounds of gunpowder and a crude timer are enough to make the world take notice. The blast, at 5:30 p.m. on July 25, killed seven people and wounded 86; it turned Paris's underground Saint-Michel station (right) into an outpost of hell, and the courtyard of Notre Dame cathedral into a landing pad for emergency helicopters. It was the worst terrorist attack to hit France since 1986— and it was only the first in a series. By year's end, explosions had injured more than 160 people; the bombings kept up in spite of strict security measures (all public trash cans were welded shut), even after police killed the prime suspect in a September shoot-out. The Armed Islamic Group, a fundamentalist faction in Algeria's civil war, took credit for the violence; they demanded that France cut its ties to the former colony's military regime. Jacques Chirac's government refused, and the terror continued.

JEAN TONGO/GAMMA LIAISON

RICK ROACH/VACAVILLE REPORTER

John Major is reelected as British prime minister. He had resigned a month earlier to show critics within his Conservative party that if an election were held, he would win it.

The **Walt Disney Company** announces plans to acquire TV conglomerate **Capital Cities/ABC** for $19 billion. Quips **Charlie Gibson,** cohost of *Good Morning America:* "I never thought I'd work for a guy named Mickey."

The board of regents of the **University of California** votes to eliminate **affirmative action** policies for faculty hirings and student admissions.

Japanese pitcher **Hideo Nomo,** who debuted with the L.A. Dodgers in May, leads the National League to a 3–2 victory in baseball's **All-Star Game.**

The FDA approves **Caverject,** the U.S.'s first prescription drug for treating impotence.

The Big Spill

Was it a disaster waiting to happen? Inspectors had reported corrosion in California's 40-year-old Folsom Dam repeatedly since 1988, but their warnings went unheeded, largely because of endless budget crunches. Then on Monday, July 17, at eight a.m., the weight of a 47-foot wall of water tore open Folsom's central spillway gate No. 3. In an instant a 6,000-cubic-feet-per-second flow jumped to a gushing 45,000. What could have been both a human and an environmental catastrophe wasn't. If the dam had broken on a weekend, 6,000 people might have been rafting and fishing on the American River; as it was, there were very few visitors, and no one was harmed. More than a third of the reservoir's water was lost, but flooding was minimal, and an unusually wet season meant the drinking-water supply was not affected. There was, however, one terrifying near miss. When the engine of a state patrol boat failed, the two lifeguards aboard jumped ship before their 22-foot cruiser was sucked through the broken gate, plummeting 300 feet into the crashing current below.

82

In a preemptive strike against an impending GOP push for **school prayer,** the Clinton administration issues guidelines on the permissibility of religious activity in public schools. Says the President: "When the First Amendment is invoked as an obstacle to private expression of religion, it is being misused." The advisory, which is sent to the nation's 15,000 public school districts, explains that voluntary participation in student-organized prayer groups is allowable; benedictions at graduation ceremonies are not.

Americans **William Barloon** and **David Daliberti,** who had been sentenced to eight years in prison for illegally crossing the Iraqi border, are released by Iraqi President **Saddam Hussein** after 114 days in captivity. The men, defense contractors working in Kuwait, had accidentally wandered into Iraq while looking for a friend at a U.N. post.

Waterworld, a futuristic action flick produced by **Kevin Costner** (who also stars), opens to mixed reviews and mediocre ticket sales. It hits Hollywood's ledger as the most expensive movie ever made. Final cost: $175 million.

A Deadly Heat

For the healthy and the affluent, it was just a sticky, sweaty, nerve-fraying annoyance. But for others, July's record-breaking heat wave—a week of 100°-plus temperatures across the Midwest and the Northeast—was a very serious matter. The weather killed more than 800 people nationwide. Most were old, infirm and unable to afford air-conditioning; many in inner-city areas were too fearful of crime to open a window. The toll was highest in Chicago, where 568 died, overwhelming ambulance services, hospitals and the county morgue, and sparking a political crisis for Mayor Richard M. Daley. (The victims had "neglected themselves," said one of his officials, answering charges of inaction.) Only in August would the last of the city's dead be laid to rest (right): 41 unclaimed bodies buried in a pauper's grave.

Aung San **Suu Kyi**

For millions of Burmese, trapped for decades under military dictatorships, Aung San Suu Kyi, 50, symbolizes the fragile hope of liberty. The Oxford-educated daughter of an independence hero—General Aung San (pictured in mural), assassinated when Suu Kyi was a toddler—she cofounded the National League for Democracy after returning to her homeland in 1988. But during a bloody crackdown, the new clique of generals running Myanmar (as they had renamed Burma) placed her under house arrest. Her party's sweeping victory in the 1990 elections did the prisoner no good, since the regime nullified the vote; neither did her 1991 Nobel Peace Prize. Confined to her crumbling villa in the capital, Yangon (formerly Rangoon), she was allowed no phone calls and only occasional visits—even from her British husband and their two grown sons, who had stayed in England. Then in July her jailers suddenly let her go. International pressure and a collapsing economy had forced the junta's hand: Myanmar needed foreign investment. Free at last after six years, the tiny woman stood on a table in her yard. "We will produce the form of government that the people want," she said, and a crowd of supporters cheered and wept. She called for moderation—"We will not bear grudges"—and negotiations. The generals, however, have declined to compromise further. Freedom for the people is not on their agenda.

Oseola McCarty, 87, a retired washerwoman from Hattiesburg, Miss., donates $150,000—a collection of dollar bills and change—to the **University of Southern Mississippi.** She makes just two requests: that the money ("more than I could ever use") fund scholarships for local black students and that she be invited to the graduation of a student helped by her gift.

Westinghouse agrees to pay $5.4 billion for **CBS,** making the TV network the last of the original three to be bought by a conglomerate.

On the *New York Times* best-seller list: the conservative treatise *To Renew America,* by **Newt Gingrich** (No. 1, nonfiction); the vampire thriller *Memnoch the Devil,* by **Anne Rice** (No. 1, fiction); and the self-help manual *Men Are From Mars, Women Are From Venus,* by **John Gray** (still No. 1 in the how-to category after 115 weeks on the list).

Fast Money

Mike Tyson's comeback had all the drama of a great boxing movie. It began in March when the former heavyweight champion left the Indiana Youth Center after serving three years for raping a beauty-pageant contestant. Tyson, once notorious for his gangsterish swagger, emerged with a new religion (Islam), a new fiancée (a medical student) and, though he still claimed innocence, a somewhat chastened attitude: "I was an ignorant person back then." He plunged into training. And soon a hulking brawler named Peter McNeeley stepped up, vowing to wrap him in a "cocoon of horror." The Don King–orchestrated August 19 match at Las Vegas's MGM Grand (right) drew a million pay-per-viewers. But the fight ended in just 89 seconds when McNeeley's manager— his client had already gone down twice— jumped in to stop it. The fans screamed "Fix," but Tyson, 29, had reason to cheer: He walked off with a record $25 million.

HOLLY STEIN/ALLSPORT

Farewell, Captain

More than any other musician, Jerry Garcia—lead guitarist and presiding spirit of the Grateful Dead—kept the outlaw optimism of the '60s alive. Known as Captain Trips during his psychedelic heyday, Garcia had mellowed, at 53, into a silver-bearded patriarch, revered by ex-hippies in business suits and by fans young enough to be his grandchildren. And when he died in August at a California drug-treatment center, his heart worn out from years of chemical abuse, legions of Deadheads (for whom the band's wild jams and cryptic lyrics are sacred texts) gave him a tearful and colorful send-off. Around the world, they put on their tie-dyed finery and gathered for communal rites, strumming guitars and singing songs of gratitude to the departed. As one mourner put it, moving through a Seattle crowd (left): "Jerry went on, but you gotta dance."

Mickey Mantle, former centerfielder and home run hitter for the New York Yankees, dies at age 63 on August 13. The hard-drinking baseball legend had been given a diagnosis of liver cancer in June and had undergone a liver transplant after only two days on the organ-donor waiting list. Doctors at Dallas's **Baylor University Medical Center** deny that their famous patient received preferential treatment. Insisting that the transplant was successful, they say Mantle's death was hastened by previously undiagnosed cancer in his lungs and abdomen.

On August 15, the 50th anniversary of Japan's surrender in World War II, Prime Minister **Tomiichi Murayama** becomes the first Japanese leader to apologize for his nation's acts during the war.

Netscape Communications, creator of a popular navigator for the World Wide Web, goes public in a frenetic stock offering that earns **Marc Andreessen,** the company's 24-year-old founder, $58 million overnight.

Chemical and **Chase Manhattan,** the nation's fourth- and sixth-largest banks respectively, announce a merger that will make them the biggest bank in America.

"I think I have always been pro-life, I just didn't know it," declares **Norma McCorvey**, a.k.a. plaintiff Jane Roe of *Roe* v. *Wade,* the 1973 Supreme Court case that legalized abortion. McCorvey, until recently marketing director at a Dallas women's health clinic, is baptized in a backyard swimming pool by Rev. **Philip Benham,** head of the antiabortion group Operation Rescue. But her "conversion," as Benham calls it, is not total: McCorvey says she still supports the abortion choice during the first trimester of pregnancy.

Two of **Saddam Hussein's** top political aides, who are also his sons-in-law, defect to Jordan with their families (two of the Iraqi leader's daughters and several of his grandchildren) and a score of other Iraqi military officials. Says **Hussein Kamel** of his father-in-law: "We will work inside Iraq and in the whole Arab world to topple the regime of Saddam."

Mortal Kombat, the movie version of the violent video game, is No. 1 at the box office in its first week. The family-friendlier *Babe,* starring a talking piglet (with a supporting cast of similarly verbal farm animals), tops out at No. 4.

Conduct Unbecoming

Shannon Faulkner spent more than two years fighting to breach the walls of South Carolina's Citadel, but her stay inside was all too brief. On August 13, thanks to a federal court order, Faulkner, 20, became the first female cadet in the elite, state-funded military academy's 153-year history. But on the opening day of Hell Week—an ordeal of nonstop marching, drilling and verbal abuse—Faulkner was one of five cadets who collapsed from the 102° heat. She languished in the infirmary, unable to hold down her food, for most of her remaining time on campus. When she quit on the 18th (by then, 22 other freshmen had dropped out), her classmates whooped with glee (right). Faulkner blamed her troubles on nerves—"All the stress I've had I just bottled up inside"—but the battle for The Citadel did not end with her defeat: Within a week, 17-year-old Nancy Mellette filed suit for the chance to take her place.

Shattered Lives

For nearly four years, Serb nationalists had dominated the three-way civil war in the former Yugoslavia—but in August the brutal tide began to turn. It happened because Bosnian Serb forces finally pushed the United Nations too far. First they overran the U.N.-protected "safe areas" of Srebrenica and Zepa, expelling Muslim families and massacring the men; then they laid siege to another safe area, Bihac. After they shelled Sarajevo's marketplace, killing some 40 people, the U.N. lashed out, authorizing a two-week NATO bombing campaign against Bosnian Serb targets— the first serious intervention aimed at ending the Balkan conflict. Croatia seized the moment to win back its Krajina region, grabbed by local Serb fighters in 1991. Now Krajina's native Serbs fled by the tens of thousands. Croat civilians stoned the refugees' buses (left) while Croatian and Bosnian Muslim troops took potshots at them and burned their homes. Reeling, Serb forces drew back from Bihac as well. And in September, as the Serbs continued to lose ground, preliminary peace talks got under way.

SEBASTIÃO SALGADO

On June 19, **Harry Wu,** a Chinese dissident and naturalized American citizen, returned to his homeland to investigate human rights abuses. Wu, who had himself endured 19 years in Chinese labor camps, was arrested on the spot and charged with espionage. His imprisonment attracted international attention and even entered White House discussions about **Hillary Clinton's** attendance at the upcoming women's conference in Beijing. On August 24, Wu is sentenced to 15 years in prison. The next day, he is suddenly released. The activist falls to his knees in gratitude upon landing in the U.S.—but his stay, he says, is temporary. "I will go back," Wu declares. "I have my blood, my tears, in Chinese soil."

Prerelease hype for **Microsoft Windows 95** included store campaigns advising buyers to reserve their copies in advance, pitches by CEO **Bill Gates,** and ads featuring the Rolling Stones song "Start Me Up." The software ($209 installed, $109 for the upgrade) goes on sale worldwide August 24 and is snapped up by more than a million computer users in just four days.

Births

Christie Brinkley, 42, divorced Billy Joel in August 1994, wed Rick Taubman, 46 (above), that December, gave birth to son Jack Paris in June and filed for divorce in July. The split, she said, "was a long time coming."

First-time mom Kim Basinger, 41, and husband Alec Baldwin, 37, welcomed daughter Ireland Eliesse into the world in October. When a paparazzo ambushed the new family on their way home from the hospital, Baldwin proved the protective dad: He decked the guy.

In June, Val Kilmer (Batman), 35, and Joanne Whalley-Kilmer (last year's TV Scarlett O'Hara), 33, had a baby, Jack. On July 21, the actress filed for divorce, citing irreconcilable differences.

& Breakups

Also born...

■ Buck, to Roseanne, 42, and new spouse Ben Thomas, 28 ■ Matalin Mary, to politicos Mary Matalin, 41, and James Carville, 50 ■ Matthew, adopted by Connie Chung, 48, and Maury Povich, 56 ■ Parker, adopted by Rosie O'Donnell, 33 ■ Twins, to a surrogate mother, for ex-couple (split in 1991) Toukie Smith, 43, and Robert DeNiro, 52, who will co-parent the boys.

■ "[We] need our own space right now. I sincerely hope this will work out," said Elizabeth Taylor, 63, about her "trial" break with seventh husband Larry Fortensky, 43.

■ Citing work as the ruin of their celebrated six-year marriage, British thespians Emma Thompson, 36, and Kenneth Branagh, 34, said, "We have drifted apart."

■ Just before the end of his 21-month marriage to Julia Roberts, 28, Lyle Lovett, 37, said: "I don't think anything I'll do in my life will be as newsworthy."

■ Jane Seymour, 44 (with hubby James Keach, 48, above), already the mother of two, added two more—twins John and Kristopher. Dr. Quinn, her TV alter ego, isn't due until 1996.

■ Israeli First Lady Leah Rabin had invited Suha Arafat, 33, to give birth in Israel. But the wife of PLO leader Yasir Arafat opted, for safety reasons, to deliver daughter Zahwa in Paris.

■ Enid Greene Waldholtz, the second congresswoman to have a baby while in office, saw marriage and career falter when she and spouse Joe were suspected of campaign fraud.

Yoko Ono, **Little Richard** and *Rolling Stone* editor **Jann Wenner** share the ribbon-cutting honors at the September 1 opening of the **Rock and Roll Hall of Fame and Museum** in Cleveland. Among the memorabilia housed in the $92 million, **I.M. Pei**-designed complex: **Bruce Springsteen's** teenage guitar, **John Lennon's** *Sgt. Pepper* jacket and a bloodstained T-shirt that belonged to Sex Pistols bassist **Sid Vicious.**

"We are not going to permit exciting new technology to be misused to exploit and injure children," declares Attorney General **Janet Reno** about the FBI's arrest of 15 people caught transmitting child pornography over **America Online.** The sting is the result of a two-year investigation called Operation Innocent Images.

Wimbledon champs **Pete Sampras** and **Steffi Graf** win again at the **U.S. Open,** but **Monica Seles,** who is defeated in the finals, proves the star of the event. It is her first Grand Slam tournament since 1993, when she was stabbed in the back by an obsessed Graf fan during a match in Hamburg, Germany.

2,131!

The clamor started in the middle of the fifth inning, when the game became official. For 20 minutes on the evening of September 6, Baltimore's Camden Yards rang with cheers (including those of Bill Clinton) as Cal Ripken Jr. circled the field, slapping fans' hands. Even players in the California Angels dugout ran out to hug him. The Orioles' affable shortstop had just broken a 56-year-old record, one that had been expected—as a plaque at Yankee Stadium put it—to "stand for all time": Lou Gehrig's 2,130 consecutive ball games. Ripken, 35, had gone 13 and a half seasons without missing a game, ignoring injuries, earning All-Star berths and securing a reputation—in an era when athletic egotism is the rule—as the ultimate team player. Although he shrugged it off ("If you could play baseball every day, wouldn't you?"), his feat restored some glory to a strike-battered sport.

WALTER IOOSS, JR./SPORTS ILLUSTRATED

ER, the hugely popular TV drama about a Chicago emergency room, wins eight **Emmy awards,** including best supporting actress (**Julianna Margulies**). The best comedy series honors go to Frasier; best drama series to NYPD Blue. Other winners include, for drama, **Mandy Patinkin** (best actor, Chicago Hope) and **Kathy Baker** (best actress, Picket Fences); for comedy, **Candice Bergen** (best actress, Murphy Brown) and **Kelsey Grammer** (best actor, Frasier). **Jay Leno,** until recently pummeled in the late-night ratings by **David Letterman,** wins his first Emmy, for The Tonight Show.

Novelist **Salman Rushdie**—in hiding since 1989, when Iran's **Ayatollah Khomeini** declared The Satanic Verses an act of blasphemy against Islam and ordered the writer found and killed—makes his first preannounced public appearance in six years at a writers' conference in London, where he promotes his new book, The Moor's Last Sigh.

In a major upset, the Europeans wrest golf's prestigious **Ryder Cup** from the U.S. team, captained by **Lenny Watkins.**

Wild Winds

Hurricane Luis swept through the eastern **Caribbean in September like a scythe, shearing the roofs off tourist villas and demolishing shantytowns. The island of St. Martin suffered some of the worst losses (right): 140-mph winds and 40-foot waves killed at least nine, left 2,000 homeless and led to widespread looting. But Luis was just one of 19 major storms that blew westward across the Atlantic this year, in the busiest hurricane season since 1933. Three of the cyclones (Allison, Erin and Opal) struck the southeastern U.S., taking 55 lives and causing more than $2 billion in property damage. Meteorologists had predicted a bumper crop of storms, citing factors ranging from warmer ocean temperatures to wet weather in Africa's Sahel desert—but foreknowledge was scant protection against the tempests' rage.**

CHRISTOPHE CALAIS/VSD

Giving in to a demand by the **Unabomber,** *The Washington Post,* at the urging of the Justice Department, publishes his 35,000-word antitechnology manifesto, "Industrial Society and Its Future." In return for the September 19 newspaper forum, the elusive terrorist promises to end the mail-bomb attacks he directs at individuals. He says his bombings of buildings, however, are likely to continue.

Miss Oklahoma (24-year-old **Shawntel Smith**) is crowned **Miss America.** Viewers of the live broadcast are asked to dial a 900 number (at 50 cents per call) to vote whether the pageant should keep its swimsuit competition. The show receives nearly a million calls. The bathing suits win, capturing 79 percent of the vote.

Time Warner announces a deal to merge with **Turner Broadcasting,** whose cable properties include CNN, the Cartoon Network and TNT. (Says billionaire **Ted Turner** about his new partnership: "I'm tired of being little for my whole life.") Also in September: Time Warner says it is selling its stake in **Interscope Records,** the label of gangsta rap stars **Snoop Doggy Dogg** and **Tupac Shakur.**

Women of the World Unite

China had lobbied hard to host the fourth United Nations World Conference on Women, a September gathering of officials from 185 countries. But Chinese authorities feared that the conference's open-admission side event, a forum of so-called NGOs (nongovernmental organizations), would be politically nettlesome. So they held the main assembly in Beijing but banished the activist forum to muddy Huairou, 90 minutes away. Yet even at the posh Beijing affair, the women pulled no punches. Hillary Rodham Clinton blasted China's forced-abortion policy (without mentioning the country by name) and insisted on the right to "assemble, organize and debate openly." In Huairou, meanwhile, despite police harassment, 25,000 women—including an Iranian TV crew (right)—had the networking session of a lifetime. They held discussions on everything from family planning to female genital mutilation. And they went home to pursue the U.N.'s call for "the full realization of all human rights" for half the world's population.

ANAT GIVON/AP

Primping for Peace

Just two years ago, only poets dreamed of this," said Israeli Prime Minister Yitzhak Rabin. On September 28—two years after their once unthinkable White House handshake—Rabin and PLO chairman Yasir Arafat were back to seal another treaty. The new accord provided a detailed plan for Israel's withdrawal from much of the West Bank; it promised limited self-rule for most of the area's Palestinians, leaving the fate of 120,000 Israeli settlers for future talks. Before the ceremony came some critical last-minute preparations by the signers (Rabin, far left, and Arafat, near right), the witnesses (Egypt's President Hosni Mubarak and Jordan's King Hussein) and President Clinton. "Enough killing," Arafat declared after putting down his pen—but five weeks later, the settler question would cost Rabin his life.

"Impossibly vulgar, tawdry and coarse, this much-touted studio splash into NC-17 waters is akin to being keelhauled through a cesspool, with sharks swimming alongside," declares a *Variety* review of *Showgirls,* the big-budget stripper flick by *Basic Instinct* screenwriter **Joe Eszterhas.**

After a 372-day trial, the *State of California* v. *Orenthal James Simpson* goes to the jury on September 29. In his fiery closing argument, defense attorney **Johnnie Cochran** focuses on racism in America and compares the tactics of L.A.P.D. detective **Mark Fuhrman** (who had been tape-recorded deriding African Americans as "niggers") to those of Hitler. "Don't be a part of this continuing cover-up. Do the right thing," Cochran charges. "If it doesn't fit, you must acquit." Prosecutor **Marcia Clark** implores the jury to look at the DNA evidence linking the former football star to the gruesome stabbing murder: "[Ron and Nicole] are telling you who did it, with their hair, their clothes, their bodies, their blood. Mr. Simpson, Orenthal Simpson, he did it. Will you hear them?"

■ Army buddies Terry Nichols, 40 (left), and Timothy McVeigh, 27, shared a hatred for the U.S. government—a sentiment that, according to their indictment, led them to "maliciously" conspire to blow up Oklahoma City's Alfred P. Murrah Federal Building.

BK 4454822 06-27-95
LOS ANGELES POLICE = HWD

BK 4454813 06-27-95
LOS ANGELES POLICE = HWD

■ Within hours of his arrest for "lewd" conduct in a car near Sunset Boulevard with streetwalker Divine Brown, Hugh Grant was front-page news—news not well received by his live-in love, model Elizabeth Hurley. Said the British actor: "I did a bad thing."

■ At the O.J. Simpson trial: Det. Mark Fuhrman (left) denied having made racist remarks; audiotapes proved otherwise. O.J.'s eternal houseguest, Kato Kaelin, thought to be the last person to see Simpson before the murders, was suspected of lying to protect his host.

■ Blind Egyptian cleric Sheik Omar Abdel Rahman, 57, was found guilty of masterminding a series of planned terrorist attacks on the United States. Chief among the violent acts: the 1993 bombing of the World Trade Center.

Crimes
&
Notoriety

From opportunism to exhibitionism, from the barbaric to the simply bizarre, 1995 had its share of moments—and people—we'd rather forget.

■ Sen. Bob Packwood resigned after 27 years in Congress when his peers voted to expel him on ethics and sexual misconduct charges. In his diaries, which were subpoenaed, the Republican had boasted of his "exploits" with female employees.

■ At the funeral of her husband of one year, J. Howard Marshall, 90, model Anna Nicole Smith, 28 (with her son, Daniel, nine), wept behind her wedding veil—and then went on to battle her 54-year-old stepson over the oil tycoon's estate.

■ In 1993, Colin Ferguson boarded a Long Island commuter train and began shooting. He killed six and wounded 19. Acting as his own attorney, he cross-examined his victims, often in rambling legalese. The judge gave him life.

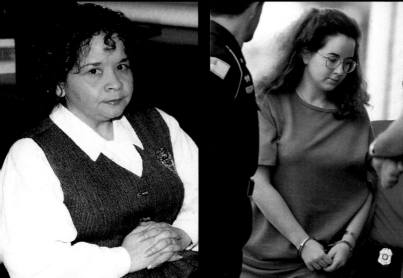

■ Yolanda Saldívar, 35, received life without parole for gunning down her former boss, Tejano star Selena, 23.

■ Her ex and the DA called for her death, but Susan Smith, 23, got life for drowning sons Michael, three, and Alex, 14 months.

And also…

■ Shoko Asahara, guru of the Aum Shinrikyo sect, indicted for the March nerve gas attack on Tokyo's subway system ■ William Aramony, ex-president of the United Way, convicted of embezzling $600,000 ■ Nicholas Leeson, 28, a Singapore-based trader accused of bankrupting Britain's prestigious Barings Bank ■ Rep. Mel Reynolds (D–Ill.), convicted of sexually assaulting a teenager ■ Calvin Klein, assailed for kiddie-pornesque jean ads, which he withdrew after a national uproar ■ Tupac Shakur, rapper, sentenced to a maximum of four years in jail for sexual assault ■ Kevin Mitnick, the FBI's most wanted hacker, charged with computer fraud

■ The FCC fined DJ Howard Stern (here hyping his book *Miss America*) $1.7 million for jokes about pedophilia and masturbation

As part of the newly signed peace accord with the PLO, **Israel** releases 900 **Palestinian** prisoners and begins its military pullout from the West Bank.

The **National Oceanic and Atmospheric Administration** unveils a new map of the ocean floor. Says one geophysicist about the **seabed chart,** which is based on once covert Navy data from the cold war era: "It's like being able to drain the oceans and look at the earth from space."

Two-parent households are on the rise for the first time in a generation, reports the **Census Bureau.** In 1994, 50.2 million Americans were **married with children**— a one-million-person increase since 1990.

The **Walt Disney Company** offers health insurance benefits to the domestic partners of its gay employees. Conservative groups assail the family entertainment giant for promoting "antifamily" values.

The Verdict

Did he or didn't he? The question had obsessed Americans since June 17, 1994, when O.J. Simpson was arrested for killing his former wife, Nicole, and her friend Ronald Goldman. Millions had followed the daily broadcasts of his trial. And on October 3, at 10:07 a.m., Los Angeles time, the nation stopped to watch the drama's conclusion. In the courtroom, the verdict brought shrieks from the victims' families and hallelujahs from Simpson's camp; elsewhere, the groans and cheers largely followed racial lines. To many whites, Simpson, 48, was a rich wife-beater who got away with murder, thanks to a legal "dream team" (F. Lee Bailey and Johnnie Cochran flanking Simpson; Robert Shapiro in rear). To a large number of blacks, he was the victim of a plot by racist police. But to the sequestered jury of 10 women and two men— nine blacks, two whites and a Latino—he was above all a defendant whose guilt had not been proved. Their deliberations took just three hours. "We were there for nine months," said a juror. "We didn't need another nine months to decide."

MYUNG J. CHUN/LOS ANGELES DAILY NEWS

A few days after his acquittal, **O.J.Simpson** agrees to a live TV interview with **Tom Brokaw** and **Katie Couric** of **NBC** (his former employer). On October 11, the day of the broadcast, Simpson, who did not take the stand during his trial, backs out. "I didn't want to be talking to Katie Clark and Tom Darden," he explains, making a dig at the prosecuting team.

Power Party

Peacekeeping failures, a swollen bureaucracy, $3.3 billion in unpaid member-nation dues: With all the United Nations' ills, detractors suggested it had little to celebrate. But over the decades, there had been triumphs, too, in famine relief, environmental protection, disease eradication, nuclear-weapons control. And so, on October 22, the U.N. pitched a 50th-birthday party—the biggest get-together of world leaders in history. Two hundred converged in New York City for three days of galas and speeches. (Each was given five minutes to address the General Assembly, though most rambled on a bit longer.) Mayor Rudolph Giuliani initiated a few skirmishes, booting Yasir Arafat from a Lincoln Center concert and barring Fidel Castro from some fancy dinners. Mostly, however, the festivities confirmed the U.N.'s central principle: Nations divided by politics, economics or ethnicity can still find ways to get along.

Amtrak's *Sunset Limited* derails in the Arizona desert, killing one and injuring nearly 100. The cause: Bolts and spikes that secured the track had been removed. Investigators at the site find several copies of a note titled "Indictment of the ATF [Alcohol, Tobacco and Firearms] and the FBI," signed by the unknown **Sons of the Gestapo.**

What's still hot? *Pulp Fiction,* 1994's film noir, now the best-selling home video of all time; Canadian singer **Alanis Morissette's** U.S. debut record, *Jagged Little Pill* (18 weeks on the charts). What's not hot? *Insomniac*, the new (unacclaimed) album from punk-pop Grammy winners **Green Day; Demi Moore** as Hester Prynne in a sexed-up version of *The Scarlet Letter.*

A Mighty Gathering

With so many black neighborhoods besieged by drugs, crime and poverty, the idea might have roused little controversy—had someone else suggested it. But the separatist doctrine and frequent anti-Semitic utterances of Nation of Islam leader Louis Farrakhan (at podium, protected by Muslim guards) made his Million Man March—a gathering of black men for "atonement and reconciliation"—a hotly debated proposition on both sides of the color line. The NAACP (whose ousted director, Benjamin Chavis, cochaired the event) and other civil rights groups withheld support. Still, on October 16, the men—837,000, according to official estimates—poured into the capital from across America. (A few women came too, though they'd been asked to stay home.) For most, the march was about something larger than Farrakhan. They hugged, sang and pledged responsibility to family and community—and Washington became, briefly, a harmonious place. "I cannot see you," said the blind musician Stevie Wonder, "but I can see your spirit."

DAVID BURNETT/CONTACT PRESS IMAGES

President Clinton signs a bill mandating stiffer penalties for crimes involving crack than for those involving cocaine. The **Congressional Black Caucus** calls the legislation unfair and "a mockery of justice," since crack users are mostly poor and black, while cocaine users are generally wealthier and white. The President says the bill is warranted because of the "violence crack fosters" but agrees to pursue similar penalties for cocaine.

Cigar becomes the first thoroughbred in 15 years to race an undefeated season when he wins the **Breeders' Cup.** The Horse of the Year's 1995 earnings: a record-breaking $4.82 million.

Conservative pundit **William Bennett,** George Bush's secretary of education, and Sen. **Joseph Lieberman** (D–Conn.) join forces against America's TV talk shows, which, Bennett says, "degrade human personality." In the fall season, a half dozen new gabfests (sample topic: nude-dancing daughters) joined the lineup. Among the **Oprah** wannabes: former *Partridge Family* member **Danny Bonaduce,** *Cosby* kid **Tempestt Bledsoe** and **Gabrielle Carteris,** late of *Beverly Hills, 90210.*

Return of the Rebels

The 2,000 guerrillas of the Zapatista National Liberation Army had been hiding in the jungles of southern Mexico since February, when government troops drove them from villages the rebels had seized in an uprising a year before. But in October a ragtag band marched out of the woods, ready to negotiate. Led by a pipe-smoking intellectual known as Subcommander Marcos (near right, on horse), the mostly Mayan Zapatistas demanded greater autonomy for the Indians of Chiapas—Mexico's poorest state—and an opening of the political process nationwide. The talks dragged through the winter with little progress. But change in Mexico seems inevitable. The economy is in free fall (despite a $20 billion U.S. bailout). Former President Carlos Salinas, accused of corruption, is in exile; his brother, charged with arranging a rival's assassination, is in jail. And after 65 years of unshakable rule, the Institutional Revolutionary Party has begun to wobble.

SCOTT SADY/AP

A Los Angeles jury makes **Clint Eastwood's** day when it finds the *National Enquirer* guilty of fabricating an interview with him. The actor-director donates his $150,000 award to charity.

The long-static U.S. labor movement is jump-started by the first contested presidential election in the **AFL-CIO's** 40-year history, when **John Sweeney,** 61, defeats a close aide of ejected president **Lane Kirkland.**

During morning exercises at North Carolina's **Fort Bragg,** Army Sgt. **William Kreutzer,** 26, opens fire on 1,300 paratroopers. Eighteen soldiers are wounded and one is killed.

After losing the **World Series** in 1991 and 1992, the Atlanta Braves win their first championship—thanks to a **David Justice** homer in the sixth game against the Cleveland Indians. Pitcher **Tom Glavine** is Most Valuable Player.

Citizens of **Quebec** reject the French-speaking province's proposal to secede from **Canada.** The vote: 50.6 percent to 49.4. Declares the federalist *Montreal Gazette:* "Canada Survives!"

A Call for Compassion

I f a papal visit can be said to have a theme, John Paul II's October U.S. tour (his fourth) was about the evils of human disunity. The journey began with a stop at Sacred Heart Cathedral (right) in poverty-stricken Newark, N.J., and included a muddy outdoor mass in New York City's **Central Park**; it ended, after five days, in Baltimore. In his opening sermon, the 75-year-old pontiff obliquely reproached the nation for its growing anti-immigrant sentiment, urging listeners not to "turn away" from newcomers. At the U.N., addressing the delegates in English, French, Russian and Spanish, he decried the spread of extreme nationalism, "which teaches contempt for other nations or cultures." And at New Jersey's Giants Stadium, he asked a rain-soaked audience of 83,000 whether a budget-cutting America is becoming "less caring toward the poor, the weak, the stranger." He did not wait for an answer: "It must not!"

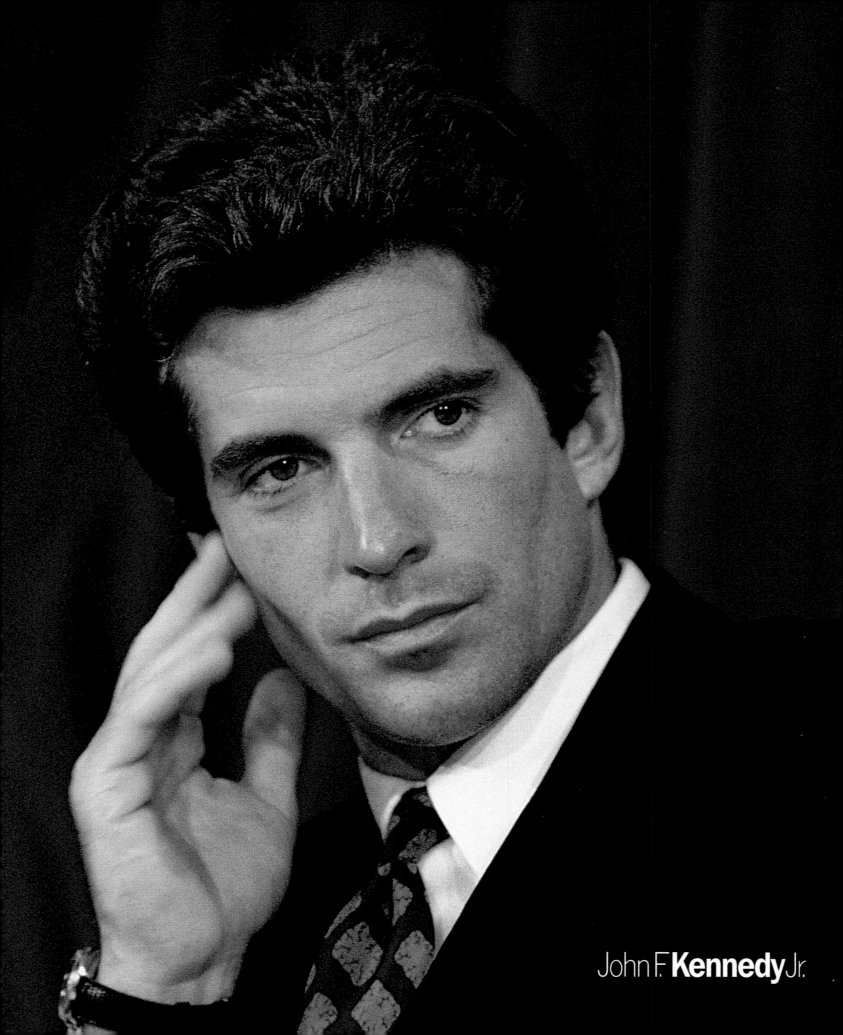

John F. **Kennedy** Jr.

H is combination of pedigree and pulchritude brings out the paparazzi whenever he skates through Central Park or busses his current love interest, Calvin Klein publicist Carolyn Bessette. But until recently the reputation of John F. Kennedy Jr. rested on a few dubious achievements: globe-trotting with actress Daryl Hannah; flunking the New York State bar exam twice; and, after passing it, spending four uneventful years as a Manhattan assistant district attorney. This year, however, Kennedy, 35, revamped himself—and in the process unveiled a new species of magazine. With partner Michael Berman, he launched *George,* a political journal infused with enough glamour to make Washington look like Hollywood East. Supermodel Cindy Crawford, costumed as the capital's namesake, graced the cover of the October debut issue; inside, Madonna pondered presidential policy, designer Isaac Mizrahi critiqued First Lady fashions, and Jackie Stallone (Sly's mom) cast electoral horoscopes. There was serious stuff, too—notably an interview by Kennedy himself with former Alabama governor (and reformed segregationist) George C. Wallace. Suddenly John-John sounded ambitious indeed. "I hope eventually to end up as president," he told a stunned gathering of potential advertisers. He let a moment pass before concluding ". . . of a very successful publishing venture."

More than 90 percent of America's senior-level managers are white males; women and minorities face "an unseen, yet unbreachable barrier that keeps [them] from rising to the upper rungs of the corporate ladder." So reports the **Glass Ceiling Commission,** led by Secretary of Labor **Robert Reich,** about its three-year study of workplace discrimination. The panel's proposal for achieving greater equity: Keep the affirmative-action hiring practices now under attack.

Citing "fundamental changes" in **the American family,** New York State's highest court rules that unmarried couples— be they heterosexual or homosexual—may adopt children. Writes Chief Judge **Judith S. Kaye:** "To rule otherwise would mean that . . . children actually being raised in homes headed by two unmarried persons could have only one legal parent, not the two who want them."

Ireland's voters nullify—by a 50.3 percent majority— their country's **constitutional ban on divorce.**

Martyred for Peace

The brigade commander who broke the siege of Jerusalem in 1948, the general who led Israel to victory in the 1967 Six Day War, Prime Minister Yitzhak Rabin had more recently traded swords for plowshares. The 1993 land-for-peace swap he engineered with the Palestinians earned him (and PLO leader Yasir Arafat) a Nobel prize—and the hatred of right-wing Jewish extremists. One of them, law student Yigal Amir, 25, was present on November 4 when Rabin addressed a Tel Aviv rally. For the first time in memory, the gruff Israeli leader sang in public, joining in the anthem "A Song for Peace." Minutes later, Amir shot him point-blank. The bloodied lyric sheet was found in Rabin's pocket. At his funeral, President Clinton, Egypt's Hosni Mubarak and a tearful King Hussein of Jordan—a foe turned friend—all spoke. But Noa Ben-Artzi Philosof, 17 (right, with her brother Yonatan), gave the most eloquent eulogy: "Grandfather, you were the pillar of fire in front of the camp, and now we are left alone, in the dark."

DENIS PAQUIN/AP

Ready— or Not?

If he were to win, Colin Powell would become America's first black President. But would he run? His wife, Alma (with him, at right), protective of her family's privacy, hoped he wouldn't. Yet millions of voters—and a host of powerful backers—hoped he would. A Horatio Alger hero from the South Bronx, Powell, 58, had proved his mettle as Ronald Reagan's National Security Adviser and as Chairman of the Joint Chiefs of Staff during the Persian Gulf war. The general (retired since 1993) was charismatic, thoughtful and reassuringly centrist—a registered independent, he called himself a "fiscal conservative with a social conscience." And he seemed free of the desperate drive that so often makes career politicians appear unprincipled or mean. Powell's months of indecision (it took him until September even to declare Republican leanings) only made him look more sincere. His memoir, *My American Journey*, topped best-seller lists; his polls topped Bill Clinton's and GOP front-runner Bob Dole's. Then, on November 8, he popped the balloon. The presidency, he said, "requires a calling that I do not yet hear."

After the **Equal Employment Opportunity Commission** orders **Hooters,** a restaurant chain staffed by scantily clad waitresses called Hooters Girls, to hire men, the company stages a protest rally. The EEOC ruling, Hooters says, is "frivolous" and "politically correct."

Navy Seaman **Marcus Gill,** 22, and Marines **Kendrick Ledet,** 20, and **Rodrico Harp,** 21—U.S. servicemen stationed on Okinawa, Japan—admit their involvement in the September kidnapping, beating and rape of a local 12-year-old girl. (The two Marines deny that they raped the child.) The crime, for which the men face possible life imprisonment, inflames a widespread sentiment among Okinawans that expiring leases on U.S. military bases should not be renewed.

When **Newt Gingrich** complains that **President Clinton** made him sit in the back of Air Force One en route to Yitzhak Rabin's funeral, the front page of the New York *Daily News* displays a caricature of the House speaker as a whining, diaper-wearing "Cry Baby." The GOP majority responds by banning the edition from the House floor. It is the first time a newspaper is so exiled.

Meet the Threetles

Since John Lennon's murder in 1980, it had seemed self-evident that a Beatles reunion, long one of pop culture's dearest dreams, would never become a reality. But time and technology can work miracles—and on November 20, 25 years after the group's bitter breakup, a new Beatles single hit the airwaves. Lennon had composed "Free As a Bird" in 1977. Eventually, Yoko Ono turned over a crude demo tape to the surviving band members (from left: George Harrison, 52, Ringo Starr, 55, and Paul McCartney, 53), whose added tracks transformed the song— an elegiac ditty about family—into an "I Am the Walrus"–style extravaganza. The release was part of a multimedia blitz: a six-hour TV documentary, a 10-hour collector's edition video, a series of CDs, even a LIFE special issue. Suddenly, as of old, the Beatles were the year's top-earning artists. Was it a happy ending for the old Fab Four or the debut of a revived Fab Three? "Think of a circle," said McCartney, cryptically. "The beginning *is* the end."

LINDA McCARTNEY

Toy Story, the first feature film to be completely animated by computer, is a blockbuster, attracting even childless adults. The voices of **Tom Hanks** and *Home Improvement*'s **Tim Allen** add star quality to the G-rated Disney flick about toys that come to life. Also in theaters: *GoldenEye,* the latest James Bond movie (No. 17), starring the latest James Bond (**Pierce Brosnan,** the fifth actor to play the part) and Dutch model **Famke Janssen** as Xenia Onatopp, an assassin who kills men by crushing them between her thighs.

Atlanta Braves pitcher **Greg Maddux,** 29, wins an unprecedented fourth consecutive **Cy Young Award.**

Mexico's **German Silva,** 27, and **Tegla Loroupe,** 22, of Kenya, win the New York City Marathon for the second straight year. His time: 2:11. Hers: 2:28.06.

The **Vatican** declares "infallible" Pope **John Paul II's** doctrine that women cannot be ordained as Roman Catholic priests.

A Federal Standstill

For six days in late November the FBI stopped training agents. The EPA quit inspecting waste sites. New passports were not to be had. And by the time the Statue of Liberty reopened (to the delight of the Malaysian tourists at right), the suspension of all "nonessential" federal services had cost taxpayers $700 million. Ironically, the fight that caused the shutdown (the ninth and longest since 1981) was over how to save money. Congress's Republican majority aimed to balance the budget within seven years, by slashing funds for welfare and other social programs, the arts and the environment. Bill Clinton's gentler plan would take nine years. November's crisis—triggered when the President vetoed a stopgap spending bill—ended only after Clinton accepted the seven-year schedule and the Republicans vaguely agreed to "protect" Medicare and Medicaid. But negotiations over the details stalled, and on December 16 the government closed up shop again.

Diana Princess of Wales

H ers is a fairy tale gone spectacularly wrong. In 1981, fresh-faced Lady Diana Spencer, then 20, wed 32-year-old Prince Charles, the heir to Britain's throne. But the bride didn't know that her groom's true love was a married horsewoman (divorced this year) named Camilla Parker Bowles, nor was she prepared for the endless invasions of privacy that come with being a royal. By the fall of 1995, the couple had been separated for nearly three years, and Diana's alleged extramarital wanderings—along with her manifold sufferings, from palace snubs to bulimia— were fodder for tabloids and best-sellers. To her adoring public, Princess Di was a lovely (if slightly dim) damsel in distress, brought to grief by a wicked (or at least insensitive) prince. On November 20, however, Diana went on the offensive. In a frank and surprisingly witty interview with the BBC, she blamed the breakup on Charles's infidelity—"there were three of us in this marriage, so it was a bit crowded"—and on his envy of her popularity. She confessed to one consolatory affair, with the dashing socialite Capt. James Hewitt. She denied any ambition to be queen, except of "people's hearts," but suggested that the succession should skip Charles and go directly to their son William. And she warned "the enemy"— her husband's backers—that she would "not go quietly." If Diana intended to force an end to her conjugal limbo without asking for it directly, the ploy worked. With the monarchy in crisis (its worst since 1936, when King Edward VIII abdicated to marry American divorcée Wallis Simpson), a fed-up Queen Elizabeth took action. In December she urged the pair to call it quits, and to do it fast.

On December 1, **World AIDS Day,** the lights of Manhattan are dimmed. Mourners in Berlin carry wooden crosses bearing the names of the dead. And on the Internet, users adorn their messages with red ribbons. The epidemic's latest statistics: 17 million HIV-infected people worldwide; four million deaths since 1981.

Two weeks later, on December 14, **Jeff Getty,** 38, receives a highly risky bone marrow transplant from a baboon. Since baboons are resistant to AIDS, scientists theorize that the untested procedure will boost Getty's HIV-weakened immune system. "I know I could die from the treatment,"says the Californian. "But I am certain I will die if I do nothing."

Chechnya begins another winter under siege, its July cease-fire with Russia having crumbled. "Every day we put something back together," says a Chechen woman in Grozny, the independence-seeking republic's capital. "And every night they blow it up again."

Keeping the Peace

The treaty ending a four-year, three-way civil war in Bosnia-Herzegovina (estimated death toll: 250,000) was signed in Paris on December 14. With Congress's reluctant approval, the first of 20,000 U.S. combat troops—part of a NATO peacekeeping force—arrived in-country just in time for the holidays. Their troubles began immediately. Blizzards delayed deployments. A flood forced the U.S. commander, Maj. Gen. William Nash, to renege on his vow to build a crucial pontoon bridge within 24 hours. And Spc. Martin Begosh, 24 (right, on stretcher, in an image captured by a TV crew), became the Yanks' first casualty, wounded by a land mine. Such logistical woes paled, however, beside the political obstacles to lasting peace. The pact—the product of a torturous November summit in Dayton, Ohio, among the presidents of Bosnia, Serbia and Croatia—made Bosnia an ungainly hybrid: a Muslim-Croat federation tied to a slightly smaller ethnic Serb republic. It satisfied none of the belligerents, whose deadly grudges fester on.

AP/APTV

During a rehearsal in New York for an HBO special, **Michael Jackson** collapses. His doctor later says the singer, who was suffering from a viral infection, may have been just 15 minutes from death.

"[I'm going to] form a ladies' sewing circle and terrorist society," jokes **Patricia Schroeder** (D–Colo.), 55, Congress's longest-serving female legislator (24 years), after announcing her retirement. Among those joining her in search of greener pastures: Rep. **Kweisi Mfume** (D–Md.), to become director of the NAACP; veteran senators **Bill Bradley** (D–N.J.), **Sam Nunn** (D–Ga.), **Mark O. Hatfield** (R–Oreg.), **Nancy Kassebaum** (R–Kans.) and **Alan K. Simpson** (R–Wyo.). Says Mfume about the mass exodus (39, all told): "Both parties are being pulled by their extremes."

In a deposition for the civil suits filed against **O.J. Simpson** by the families of **Ronald Goldman** and **Nicole Brown Simpson**, actress **Paula Barbieri** testifies that she left O.J. a Dear John phone message on the morning of the murders. During his trial, Simpson's lawyers suggested that nothing upsetting or unusual had happened to their client that day.

Slip-Sliding Away

A few hours before dawn on December 11, sleepers in San Francisco's posh Sea Cliff section were awakened by fire engines. The problem was not fire, however, but water. A century-old brick sewer main had collapsed during a rainstorm, spewing a torrent that liquefied the sandy soil around it. Soon a crater 200 feet wide by 100 deep was gnawing at the neighborhood's heart. And at six a.m., the great mouth claimed a victim—an 85-year-old, $2.6 million mansion (left). Luckily, the house was vacant. But the sinkhole menaced more than 20 other structures, including the boyhood home of photographer Ansel Adams. (In one real-life cliffhanger, a family rescued valuables as a crane kept their house from toppling into the abyss.) It took a week to fill the pit, partly with debris from the city's 1989 earthquake. Unlike that disaster, this one may have been avoidable: Residents charged that the sewer pipe had been damaged during the construction of a drainage tunnel nearby.

The Senate votes 54–44 to ban so-called "partial birth" abortion, a rare late-term procedure used principally in life-threatening medical emergencies. The legislation (a similar version of which the House passed 288–139) marks the first time since the 1973 *Roe* v. *Wade* decision that Congress has voted to outlaw a method of abortion. **President Clinton,** who vows to veto the bill, is still, at year's end, without a replacement for ousted Surgeon General **Joycelyn Elders.** Clinton's nominee, ob-gyn **Henry Foster,** was rejected by the Senate in June because of his professional history, which included performing abortions.

TPA, a drug used to dissolve blood clots, is found to help prevent irreversible brain damage in **stroke victims.**

Jane Austen is all the rage. First, there was *Clueless*—a comedy based on the Austen novel *Emma*—starring newcomer **Alicia Silverstone** as a trendy L.A. teen. Then moviegoers flocked to a Hollywood version of *Persuasion*. Now, in December, *Sense and Sensibility* (adapted for the screen by its star, **Emma Thompson**) is a hit. Coming to television in 1996: the BBC's *Pride and Prejudice.*

A Cold Conclusion

Winter hit America early, and it hit stunningly hard. On December 11, an arctic cold wave blasted the country's eastern half, killing nearly three dozen people from Wisconsin to Georgia; in normally sultry Baton Rouge, La., the mercury plunged to a record 23°. Eight days later, a massive storm dumped up to 15 inches of snow on an area stretching from the Midwest to New England. The whiteout didn't stop mail deliveries in Auburn, Maine, (right)— but it stranded thousands of holiday travelers at airports and put a damper on already sluggish Christmas retail sales. To shivering optimists, the frigid weather had a positive side: It seemed to give the lie to warnings of global warming. But when all the numbers were tallied, they furnished little comfort. For the planet as a whole, scientists say, the average temperature for 1995 (59°, give or take a degree) was the hottest since 1856— the first year for which records exist.

"Boy, it was neat that Forrest Gump became an astronaut."
—**Small boy, exiting** *Apollo 13*

"I'm a slimeball in it, but at least it's not a big part."
—**Henry Kissinger, about how he is portrayed in the Oliver Stone film** *Nixon*

"[Keanu] Reeves remembered his lines . . . and he does look great in tights."
—**Theater review in the Toronto** *Globe and Mail,* **of a local production of** *Hamlet*

"Nothing. I live in a hut in Tibet."
—**Richard Gere, answering a** *Premiere* **magazine query about what props he has kept from his movie roles**

"I had no idea the thing was televised. Boy, is my face red now."
—**David Letterman, after flopping as host of the Academy Awards**

"What a pathetic woman. She's in a dead-end marriage, so what does she do? She has an affair." "What should she have done?" "She *could* have taken a class."
—**Overheard conversation between two women about Francesca, the protagonist of** *The Bridges of Madison County,* **starring Clint Eastwood and Meryl Streep**

"Yes! Yes! Yes! [We're just] normal—I know it's hard to believe—people."
—**Lisa Marie Presley-Jackson, when asked by** *PrimeTime Live's* **Diane Sawyer whether she and husband Michael Jackson do "the thing"**

"There's never been a time in my life where I've felt less inclined to get married."
—**Elizabeth Hurley, Estée Lauder model, about her plans to wed her longtime boyfriend, actor Hugh Grant (who was arrested in June for soliciting sex from a prostitute).**

"Women have to work harder [than men], look better and always be in a good mood."
—**Rosario Green, the highest ranking woman executive at the United Nations**

"If the B-2 is invisible, just announce you've built a hundred of them and don't build them."
—**Rep. John Kasich (R–Ohio), protesting further production of the stealth bomber**

"Why is it that Republicans can spend ten days on the Waco hearings, eight days on the Ruby Ridge hearings, twenty-four days on the Whitewater hearings, but when it comes to Medicare, there are no days for hearings?"
—**Sen. Tom Daschle (D–S.Dak.)**

"I find this process, where my hands are tied by a law signed by Ulysses S. Grant, increasingly distasteful."
—**Bruce Babbitt, secretary of the interior, about having to approve the sale, for $275, of 110 acres of federal land in Idaho believed to contain minerals worth as much as $1 billion**

"The women's movement has been through tougher things than this."
—**Donna Shalala, secretary of health and human services, about being jostled by Chinese soldiers in Beijing at the U.N. Conference on Women**

"I looked like $6 million— but they were paying me $12 million."
—**Demi Moore, mother of three and star of the upcoming** *Striptease,* **about her new hard body, which she displayed on the** *Late Show with David Letterman*

"A guy with Peaceable Texans for Guns called me the other day to say he was going to kill me."
—**State legislator Keith Oakley, who supports the right of his fellow Texans to carry concealed weapons, about threats made against him because he favors putting the issue to a public vote**

"Three dresses, I must be a Republican."
—**Comedian Brett Butler, host of the Ford's Theatre Presidential Gala, about her multiple costume changes during the evening**

"My mother once said I should never give a talk after seven at night, especially if I'm tired, and she sure turned out to be right."
—**President Clinton, after telling a gathering of Democratic contributors in Texas that he had raised taxes too much**

"There is too much hitting, too much shooting, too much violence, too much yelling. It's the kind of society you would have sent missionaries to in the 19th century."
—**William Bennett, former secretary of education, about television talk shows**

"The arts are not going to die in America because Congress turns its back on them—the artist is a weed that can survive in the cracks of a sidewalk."
—**Playwright Arthur Miller, in a letter to House Speaker Newt Gingrich**

"It exceeds the bounds of immoral acts."
—**Beijing's** *People's Daily,* **deploring a rise in the theft of manhole covers**

"There was a woman . . . Had a jacket that was sort of two-thirds unbuttoned . . . showing, as best as I could tell, bare breasts . . . I was so fascinated in watching her bid and play that I could hardly concentrate on the breasts."
— **Diary entry of Sen. Bob Packwood (R–Oreg.), who resigned after a Congressional ethics committee found him guilty of sexual misconduct and other abuses of power, about a female bridge player**

"She's just fighting [in] her corner and doing it well, with those tanned, big, muscled arms in sleeveless dresses, the slicked-back hair. She's saying, 'I'm a woman in control. I'm Schwarzenegger.'"
— **Jane Procter, editor of the British monthly *Tatler,* about Princess Diana**

"It would be the equivalent of having the prime minister of England invite the Oklahoma City bombers to 10 Downing Street, to congratulate them on a job well done."
— **Margaret Thatcher, former British prime minister, about President Clinton's warm welcome of Sinn Fein leader Gerry Adams**

"We've never had a President named Bob. And I think it's time."
— **Sen. Bob Dole (R–Kans.), 72, about his run for the White House**

"I still have my Ferrari, I still have my Bentley, I still have my home in Brentwood and my apartment in New York."
— **O.J. Simpson, explaining that his legal bills had not left him broke**

"Lawyer to O.J.: I have good news and bad news. What do you want to hear first? O.J.: The bad news. Lawyer: The bad news is that it is your blood all over the crime scene, that the DNA proves it. O.J.: Well, so what's the good news? Lawyer: The good news is that your cholesterol is only 130."
— **Joke told by Lance Ito, presiding judge at O.J. Simpson's murder trial, to defense attorney Johnnie Cochran**

"Nobody's perfect."
— **Johnnie Cochran, about the times police were called to stop client O.J. Simpson from beating his wife, murder victim Nicole Brown Simpson**

"She's a bitch."
— **Kathleen Gingrich, mother of the House speaker, whispering her son's opinion of First Lady Hillary Rodham Clinton to TV newswoman Connie Chung**

"I have made far more money by allowing my ego to rule my instincts than I ever would have by figuring the bottom line alone."
— **Millionaire developer Donald Trump, about his recipe for success**

"It's not just because he didn't invite me to dinner, but because on my way into town from the airport there were such enormous potholes."
— **Fidel Castro, explaining why he wouldn't vote for New York Mayor Rudolph Giuliani, who barred him from several events during the U.N.'s 50th-anniversary celebrations**

"I want to find out who this FICA guy is and how come he's taking so much of my money."
— **Nick Kypreos, a Canadian forward for the New York Rangers, on what he hoped to learn during his hockey team's visit to the White House**

"He's a Polack. They're very antiwomen."
— **Ann Landers, to *The New Yorker,* about Pope John Paul II. The advice columnist later apologized for her bigotry.**

"[He] compares a person who speaks racism to Hitler, who murdered millions of people? This man is a horror."
— **Fred Goldman, father of the murdered Ronald Goldman, about attorney Johnnie Cochran's assessment of racist detective Mark Fuhrman**

"I'm a brand."
— **Martha Stewart's self-assessment**

"We have A, B and C table manners."
— **Sarah Ferguson, Duchess of York, explaining the gradation of manners she has taught her daughters, princesses Beatrice and Eugenie, for "tea with Granny," for eating in public and for eating at home**

"I don't care how much of a lama he is, he still needs his mother. The monks are spoiling him rotten, and he is turning into a little tyrant rather than a little Buddha."
— **Maria Torres, of Bubión, Spain, whose 10-year-old son, Osel, is believed by Tibetan monks to be a reincarnated lama**

"How you die is the most important thing you ever do. . . . I've been waiting for this for years."
— **Timothy Leary, 74, former Harvard psychologist and LSD advocate, when informed that he had inoperable prostate cancer**

"I have always believed that most people want peace and are ready to take a risk for it."
— **Israeli Prime Minister Yitzhak Rabin, moments before his assassination**

Ginger**Rogers**

DANCER-ACTRESS 83

How gracefully she dipped and spun
in Fred Astaire's elegant embrace!
But there was substance beneath
the froth, and her 1940 Oscar for
Kitty Foyle proved it.

Late Greats

It seemed they were always part of our lives. We marveled at their talents, laughed at their antics, celebrated their remarkable achievements: the baseball hero who always swung for the fences; the matriarch who gave birth to an American dynasty; the statesman who dared to shake hands with his former foes. No matter that few of us had ever met the people on these pages. Their spirit and grace touched our hearts. And we will miss them.

1937 MUSEUM OF MODERN ART/FILM STILLS ARCHIVE

Lana**Turner**

ACTRESS 75

The Sweater Girl's impressive performances in films like *The Postman Always Rings Twice* and *Peyton Place* weren't nearly as dramatic as her offscreen life: seven husbands, a suicide attempt and the stabbing death of mobster boyfriend Johnny Stompanato, who was killed by the movie queen's 14-year-old daughter during a domestic argument.

Mickey**Mantle**

BASEBALL PLAYER 63

Though the beloved Yankee slugger's battles with alcohol proved him all too human, he always seemed larger than life. A quarter century after his last at bat, the Mick still holds the mark for the longest home run: 565 feet.

141

Louis**Malle**

D I R E C T O R   63

Wealth he had: The Frenchman was the heir to a sugar fortune. Fame he earned: *The Silent World,* a documentary he directed with Jacques Cousteau, won an Oscar in 1953. And more than 20 films— the controversial *Pretty Baby,* the elegiac *Atlantic City,* the revealing *Au Revoir les Enfants*—secured his artistic reputation on both sides of the Atlantic.

1994 CATHERINE CABROL/GLMR

Warren**Burger**

C H I E F   J U S T I C E   87

To Richard Nixon's consternation, his first Supreme Court appointment ruled in favor of school busing and abortion rights—and also decreed that the White House turn over presidential tapes for use in the Watergate investigation.

1984 NEIL LEIFER

Howard**Cosell**

S P O R T S C A S T E R   77

By his own admission "arrogant, pompous, obnoxious, verbose," the former attorney held court at landmark fights (Ali vs. Frazier in '71) and for 14 years on *Monday Night Football.*

1983 © ARNOLD NEWMAN

Jerry**Garcia**

M U S I C I A N   53

Truckin' through the '60s on into the '90s, Captain Trips kept flower-child idealism alive for Deadheads—including many who had turned in their tie-dyed tees for pinstriped suits.

1993 ©MARK SELIGER/OUTLINE PRESS

143

Yitzhak**Rabin**

ISRAELI PRIME MINISTER 73

Triumphant general of the Six Day War
of 1967—and of the current campaign
for peace—he was assassinated by a
countryman unable to abandon the
legacy of hate.

Jonas**Salk**

SCIENTIST 80

His development of a safe polio vaccine in 1955 essentially put an end to the crippling disease that attacked the young and killed thousands each year. During the last decade of his life, he turned his attention to another epidemic: AIDS.

William**Kunstler**

ATTORNEY 76

Defender of the Black Panthers and the Chicago Seven (here with Jerry Rubin), the flamboyant champion of controversial causes enraged many who accused him of grandstanding. But he never backed down from his self-appointed mission "to keep the state from becoming all domineering, all powerful."

Elizabeth**Montgomery**

A C T R E S S   62

A Hollywood brat (dad was the actor Robert Montgomery), her many charms cast a spell on viewers of the '60s sitcom *Bewitched*. Later dramatic roles never stopped fans from seeing her as the extraordinary housewife with the cute button nose.

James**Herriot**

A U T H O R   78

In books like the best-selling *All Creatures Great and Small* and *Every Living Thing,* the Yorkshire veterinarian told heartwarming tales of pigs and puppies and their owners. Translated into 20 languages, his stories delighted readers worldwide.

Selena

S I N G E R   23

As Selena Quintanilla Perez was poised to cross the Tex-Mex border into the mainstream of American culture, the beloved Tejano music star was forever silenced, shot dead by the founder of her fan club.

Harold**Wilson**

BRITISH PRIME MINISTER 79

His pragmatic ability "to get on with the job" kept the rumpled, pipe-smoking Labour Party leader in the political forefront during the '60s and '70s.

1960 JOHN SADOVY

Margaret Chase **Smith**

CONGRESSWOMAN 97

A fixture on Capitol Hill for 32 years, the "lady from Maine" was renowned as the conscience of the Senate and the first woman elected to both houses of Congress.

1956 ALFRED EISENSTAEDT

Krissy**Taylor**

MODEL 17

Despite more than a dozen magazine covers to her credit, the Florida teen lived at home and hung out with high school pals. Her sudden death raised the specter of drug use, but it was asthma that caused the fatal collapse.

1993 ©MIKEL ROBERTS/SYGMA

Eazy-**E**

RAPPER 31

Eric Wright was just another homeboy out of south-central L.A. until 1988, when he produced N.W.A.'s landmark album, *Straight Outta Compton*. Before he died of AIDS, the hip-hop father of eight warned others against unsafe sex.

1992 © ED ESPOSITO

J.William**Fulbright**

CONGRESSMAN 89

During a legislative career that spanned three decades, the chairman of the powerful Senate Foreign Relations Committee was for the U.N., against Vietnam and behind the fellowships that enabled thousands to study in Europe.

1960 MICHAEL ROUGIER

Maggie**Kuhn**

ACTIVIST 89

The Gray Panthers founder championed the elderly at work (toppling mandatory-retirement laws) and at play (advocating "sex until rigor mortis sets in").

1981 SCOTT STEWART/AP

Rose Fitzgerald
Kennedy

MATRIARCH 104

The woman behind America's
star-crossed political dynasty
regarded her life as a succession
of "agonies and ecstasies,"
which an unwavering faith helped
her to endure with dignity.

Ida L**

ACTRESS-DIRE

She worked bot
camera: as an act
like 1940's *They D*
and as one of Ho
fem

Peter**Cook**

C O M E D I A N 57

Before Monty Python crossed the
Atlantic, this edgy comic, a star
of the hilarious '60s revue *Beyond the
Fringe* and editor of the satiric
magazine *Private Eye,* brought British
comedy to the Colonies.

Wolfman**Jack**

D I S C J O C K E Y 57

Late at night, Robert Smith's raspy voice
implored listeners to *"put your hands on
the radio and feeeel me."* They did—on more
than 2,200 stations around the world.

AlexanderGodunov

DANCER-ACTOR 45

After soaring to fame in the Bolshoi Ballet, he defected to the U.S., where his dance career stumbled. Star turns in *Witness* and *Die Hard* followed, but his hard drinking brought it all to an end.

Pancho**Gonzalez**

TENNIS PLAYER 67

A fiery competitor, with smoking good looks and a serve to match, the Lone Wolf came up aces in the '40s and '50s.

Bobby**Riggs**

TENNIS PLAYER 77

No one did more for women's tennis than the brash self-promoter who challenged Billie Jean King in the 1973 Battle of the Sexes— and lost. By then he'd become such a hustler it was easy to forget how great he had been: Riggs won Wimbledon in 1939.

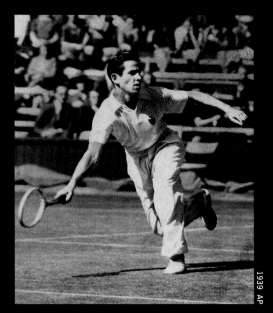

Fred**Perry**

TENNIS PLAYER 85

Stylish on and off the court, Britain's greatest player ever sealed his reputation as the Beau Brummell of the sport by founding the classic clothing line bearing his name.

Dean**Martin**

SINGER-ACTOR 78

The suave Dino Crocetti was a perfect foil
for comedy partner Jerry Lewis's antics.
After their breakup, the boozy Rat Packer
won respect for his dramatic work
(The Young Lions, Some Came Running)
in a 55-film career. His "Everybody
Loves Somebody" sent women
swooning—and stole the No. 1 spot
from the Beatles in 1964.

Sergei**Grinkov**

ICE-SKATER 28

The romantic style that won two Olympic golds for the handsome Muscovite and his wife, Ekaterina Gordeeva, led observers to say that their two hearts beat as one. But his betrayed him during a practice in Lake Placid. He died on the ice, his love at his side.

Bessie**Delany**

AUTHOR 104

A Harlem dentist whose father was a freed slave, she wrote, with her older sister Sadie, the 1993 best-seller *Having Our Say: The Delany Sisters' First 100 Years.* Late in life—very late—the sisters became the toast of Broadway when their story was turned into a hit play.

Burl**Ives**

SINGER-ACTOR 85

The barrel-chested folksinger ("Jimmy Crack Corn") was also a formidable actor, winning raves as Big Daddy in *Cat on a Hot Tin Roof,* an Oscar for 1958's *The Big Country.* and the love of children as the narrator on TV's annual airing of *Rudolph the Red-Nosed Reindeer.*

George**Abbott**

SHOWMAN 107

When the lights finally dimmed for Mr. Broadway, the actor/writer/director/ producer had worked his magic on more than 120 shows—*Sweet Charity, The Pajama Game, Damn Yankees,* to name a few.

Butterfly **McQueen**

ACTRESS 84

The line "I don't know nothin' 'bout birthin' babies" immortalized her as Prissy, Scarlett's high-strung maid in *Gone With the Wind.* But nixing servant roles put an end to her film career. An antipoverty activist, and a college grad at 64, Thelma McQueen died alone and destitute, of burns suffered in a fire at her tiny Georgia cottage.

Eva**Gabor**

ACTRESS 74

Zsa Zsa's younger sister (with the equally unforgettable Hungarian accent) won the hearts of TV viewers as the ditzy, city-bred farmwife in *Green Acres.* A shrewd businesswoman, she also ran a multimillion-dollar wig company.

FAREWELL TO SERVICEMEN, PENNSYLVANIA STATION, NEW YORK CITY, 1943

Alfred**Eisenstaedt**

Born 1898. A refugee from Nazi Germany, he came to the newborn LIFE in 1936—and never left. Eisie inspired generations of photojournalists. Tiny, quick-witted and relentlessly curious, armed with a simple Leica and a superb feel for natural light, he could tell a complex story in a single shot. He captured the dramas of ordinary folk and pierced the masks of the famous—from Hitler to Dietrich to Clinton.

Dmitri**Kessel**

Born 1902. A farmer's son from the Ukraine, Kessel started shooting for LIFE in 1937. He made his mark as a World War II combat photographer; later his subjects ranged from European royalty to African miners. During a seven-month assignment in China, his omnivorous lens caught this view of the Yangtze River.

WUSHAN GORGE, CHINA, 1946

George**Rodger**

Born 1908. Hired by LIFE in 1939, Rodger covered the Blitz in his native England, then followed the fighting around the globe. But after recording the horrors of the newly liberated Bergen-Belsen concentration camp, he gave up war photography for good. He went on to create celebrated portraits of Africa's Nuba wrestlers and Masai herdsmen and to cofound the Magnum photo agency.

BOY WALKS PAST CORPSES AT BERGEN-BELSEN, GERMANY, 1945

DUCK SWIMMING IN DETERGENT, 1951

Albert**Fenn**

Born 1912. The son of a Broadway actress and a physics professor, Fenn saw photography as "a mixture of science and art." Working for LIFE from 1941 to 1962, he covered polar expeditions, the space race— and, in 1951, this buoyancy experiment with one unhappy duck.

FIVE GENERATIONS OF AN OZARK FAMILY, 1948

Nina**Leen**

Born c. 1910. Russian émigré Leen was a well-known animal photographer when she joined LIFE in 1945. Soon she was training her naturalist's eye on human subjects—such as this Ozark farm family. The 1948 photo is one of the images of life on earth aboard the *Voyager* space probes.

A **Star** Is Born

Newt, Michael, Di, Madonna, Cal, Paul, George and Ringo. We call these people stars. Some much-needed perspective: 7,000 light-years away, in the Eagle Nebula, real stars are born. In 1995 the Hubble Space Telescope sent back photographs of this act of creation. No star on earth ever shone so bright.